MORAL RESPONSIBILITY

MORAL RESPONSIBILITY

Christopher Cowley

ACUMEN

Františce a Elišce

Acumen Publishing Limited
4 Saddler Street
Durham
DH1 3NP, UK

ISD, 70 Enterprise Drive
Bristol, CT 06010, USA

www.acumenpublishing.com

ISBN: 978-1-84465-564-9 (hardcover)
ISBN: 978-1-84465-565-6 (paperback)

British Library Cataloguing-in-Publication Data
A catalogue record for this book is available from the British Library.

Typeset in Warnock Pro.
Printed and bound in the UK by
CPI Group (UK) Ltd, Croydon, CR0 4YY.

CONTENTS

ACKNOWLEDGEMENTS

This book is designed for upper-level undergraduates and masters students as a wide-ranging and occasionally provocative introduction to some of the philosophical problems surrounding the concept of moral responsibility. It also introduces students to some of the philosophers and literature that explore these problems in much greater detail.

I would like to gratefully acknowledge permission to use material from two published articles: The section "Forgiveness", in Chapter 3, draws from my "Why Genuine Forgiveness Must be Elective and Unconditional", *Ethical Perspectives* 17(4) (December 2010) and Chapter 8 "Learning to Love", draws from my "Learning to Love", *Philosophical Topics* 38(1) (Spring 2011). I want to thank Timothy Chappell who read the entire manuscript and commented on it in great and generous detail. Among his comments was a strong objection to an argument I deploy in Chapter 8, and I have tried to reproduce that objection in order to respond to it. David Levy has helped me on a number of occasions in matters relating to the content of this book. Alan Greene helped me with a lot of the legal material. Finally, the most direct personal influence on this book was from Marina Barabas, of the Czech Academy of Sciences, in Prague. It was she who first suggested the topic to me, and we have discussed most of the problems in the book at some point in the past few years. All the best insights are probably hers, but it would have been tedious to reference them all properly. I thank her for her help, and for her continuing friendship.

INTRODUCTION

C'est le temps que tu as perdu pour ta rose qui fait ta rose si importante.

C'est le temps que j'ai perdu pour ma rose … fit le petit prince, afin de se souvenir.

Les hommes ont oublié cette vérité, dit le renard. Mais tu ne dois pas l'oublier. Tu deviens responsable pour toujours de ce que tu as apprivoisé. Tu es responsable de ta rose …

Je suis responsable de ma rose … répéta le petit prince, afin de se souvenir.

(Antoine de Saint-Exupéry, *Le Petit Prince*, ch. 21)[1]

It is one of my earliest childhood memories. I am about five years old, seated on a normal (adult) chair at a wooden table, the edge of the table barely under my chin. On the table is a plastic cup, lying on its side. Around the cup is a large puddle of milk, which, given the table's slight incline, is dripping off the right-hand side of the table onto the white linoleum floor. There is nobody else in the room.

I stare at the cup in fascinated terror. For it was me who knocked the cup over. And my mother would be returning in a moment and she would *know* I did it. She's too clever, our mum, she knows cups don't spill themselves, she knows birds can't fly in through closed windows to tip cups over, she would not have felt the earthquake that shook the table, cup and milk. What was I going to do? What was I going to say? I started sobbing. In she came, huge and strong, lumbering in slow motion; she looked at the milk, she looked at me, she scowled her terrible scowl, and all I could say was "Santa did it".

The concept of responsibility is one of the most primitive moral concepts, one of the most familiar. Even if a five-year-old might not understand the word "responsibility", he sure understands the expressions "it's her fault" and "it's not my fault", the expressions "I'm sorry" and "well done", he understands the threat and the reality of punishment (punishment *for* something), and he understands that Mum's terrible scowl expects some sort of explanation of what happened. The primitiveness and familiarity of the concept is very important for this book; this is not a book about some obscure technical subject only of interest to philosophers. This is a book about a fundamental part of what it means to be human beings and to have moral relations with other human beings. At the same time, the concept of responsibility is a lot more complicated when we start to look at it closely.

THE MANY MEANINGS OF RESPONSIBILITY

Retrospective responsibility

In philosophy, it is often helpful to examine the etymology of a complicated word in order to better understand its wider meanings and resonances. In this I follow John Lucas (1970: ch. 2). "Responsibility" clearly has something to do with a *response*; but more specifically, a response to *someone*.[2] Whenever we talk about responsibility, therefore, there is the person (we might call him an agent) who may or may not *be* responsible, who may or may not *feel* responsible, and there is the other person (we can call him the observer), who is *holding* the agent responsible for a *fault*, and who may or may not be *justified* in holding him responsible. Feeling responsible will normally result in some sort of explanation, or *excuse*, or *apology*. There are many ways of holding someone responsible, both in a positive and a negative way: admiration, contempt, delight, ridicule, gratitude, resentment, forgiveness, and above all praise and *blame*, and reward and *punishment* – what Peter Strawson calls the "reactive attitudes". All these italicized words are inter-related, and all of them will have to be discussed in this book.

Moreover, there is the thing the agent is responsible *for*: in our first example, it was an event, the spilling of the milk. The concept of agency already implies the capacity to cause changes in the world, intentionally or unintentionally. So we might schematize the milk-spilling by saying: the agent A is responsible for an event X to an observer B. But right away we have to be careful, because responsibility can mean no more than *causal* responsibility, and this has no essential connection either to moral responsibility, or indeed to human agency: the blocked carburettor is (causally) responsible for the car's breakdown. When I "blame" the carburettor, this is in a diagnostic sense and not in a moral sense – and it would not make sense to resent (a moral concept) the carburettor for failing. And even when someone spills the milk, this might not have any moral implications, in the sense that it might not be anybody else's business what that person does with his milk. Nor is causal responsibility a necessary condition for moral responsibility; I can reasonably be held responsible for things I did not do, precisely because I *should have* done them.

As an intuitive test, then, moral responsibility – the subject of this book – begins when an observer is inclined to experience and express reactive attitudes towards the agent for some aspect of the agent's relationship with his environment, namely what he did, intentionally or unintentionally, or failed to do. Importantly, holding responsible in this first view is essentially *retrospective*; the question is about the agent's past conduct. My mother enters the room and the milk is already spilt. She wants to know what happened and how. What is interesting here is that while the act was in the past – the milk has spilled and is lost for ever – the ownership of the act continues into the present; and the child is inculcated into seeing the act as if it were continually and unavoidably present in his ownership. The child learns to admit to causal responsibility, and learns to apologize for moral responsibility. This type of moral responsibility has traditionally been of greatest interest to the law, of course, as well as to philosophers. The whole business of police investigation, trial and punishment is a way of coming to terms now, in the present, with something bad that happened in the past.

Part I of this book will therefore be about this retrospective responsibility. We will begin by examining the basic schema of event, agent and accuser, together with the bilateral "blame game" that goes on between accuser and agent. Holding the agent responsible is not the end of the story here, but the beginning of a "conversation" between the two: the agent (if treated fairly) can offer new information or arguments as part of a defence, and then the accuser can evaluate the quality of that defence. Two such defences we shall consider (in Chapter 1) are duress and provocation. In both cases the agent (or defendant in the legal context), while accepting causal responsibility, is denying that he is as morally responsible as it might have appeared to the accuser at first. In Chapter 2, I then consider responsibility for unintended mistakes, especially those arising from recklessness and negligence. On the face of it, both concepts present a problem for the accuser: in the paradigmatic cases of intentional actions, blame for the action can be "pinned" on the agent's intention, but with recklessness and negligence there does not seem to be anything comparable in the agent's mind to pin the blame on. The reckless agent lacked the required appreciation of known risks, and the negligent agent lacked the required knowledge, care or attention; but both agents, given their mindsets at the moment of action, were not really free to have done otherwise – and therefore not morally responsible. Chapter 3 moves to the next stage of one of the branches of the blame game: the agent accepts causal *and* moral responsibility, and indeed feels badly enough about it to apologize. As we shall see, however, the notion of an apology is more complicated than a mere explanation, especially when the relationship between agent and act is ambiguous. At the very least, however, it seems to comprise a request for forgiveness; upon the presentation of the offender's apology, the victim (who may have been the original accuser) then has to decide whether to forgive, and under what conditions.

Forgiveness is one response to the wrong, and it is only available to the victim in an interpersonal context. Punishment is another response to the wrong, and it is only available to an appropriate institutional authority (family, club, organization, and especially the state), once it has considered and justifiably rejected any defences offered by the defendant. Both forgiveness and punishment presuppose that the agent is morally responsible for the wrong. Punishment involves attempting to make her *experience* the full extent of that responsibility, or so I shall argue in Chapter 4. The final chapter of Part I, Chapter 5, concerns the topic of "moral luck". So many of the offences for which we might hold ourselves or be held responsible seem to depend to an uncomfortable degree on good or bad luck. Two drivers set off on their journeys equally recklessly, but only one of them kills a pedestrian who strayed into his path: one will be held responsible for manslaughter and sent to prison, while the other will be held responsible only for dangerous driving. This seems to go directly against a widespread conception of morality as being *immune to luck*. I examine the different forms of luck, and ask to what degree this might challenge our understanding of moral responsibility.

Prospective responsibility

Moral responsibility can also be prospective, forward-looking,[3] and this is what I shall consider in Part II of the book. The most obvious form of prospective responsibility is that associated with a role, but this can actually mean two things. In the first meaning, a responsibility is a loose synonym for a duty attached to a role. A job description comprises a list of responsibilities (usually specific hypothetical actions) which the job-holder then agrees to discharge, and which can form the basis of a later accusation of failure of negligence. The second meaning of prospective responsibility is much more interesting, and will occupy us for Part II of the book. The role occupant is responsible *for someone*, for looking after them, for meeting their future needs, precisely in virtue of occupying the role. This type of responsibility has been of much less interest to philosophers than retrospective responsibility.

As my paradigm examples in Chapter 6, I take the doctor and the parent, and I explore what it means for a "good" doctor or parent to be responsible for their patient or child respectively. Part of what it means for the doctor, I argue, is the degree to which the agent conceives of and identifies with her role beyond that defined by the employment contract. In the case of the good parent, there is a further question of whether the parent's responsibility can or should be unconditional, and in what sense. In Chapter 7, I then consider the "role" of *human being*, and ask what it might mean to be responsible for strangers, simply in virtue of their status as fellow human beings. The obvious example here is that of the Good Samaritan. But I also take Mark Twain's character of Huckleberry Finn, and especially the scene where he deceives the slave-hunters about the identity of the runaway slave Jim. This example is philosophically interesting precisely because it involves one person taking responsibility for another, but *without explicit reasons*; indeed, Huck acts explicitly against the reasons generated by his racist conscience.

The final chapter, Chapter 8, will look at the possibility of taking responsibility not so much for another person as for oneself, and for one's life, in an adverse situation, and especially in a situation that one considers *permanent*. I have in mind two examples of adversity, the first that of a prisoner falsely sentenced to life in prison, and the second that of a devout Catholic housewife who has grown to dislike her husband but who cannot seriously contemplate leaving him. Now, of course the prisoner could try to escape, or to clear his name, or to fight and protest the injustice at every step. But another option would be to accept that he is trapped, and instead of "sulking" (his word) through the rest of his life, he can try to make as much as he can of the limited options available to him in the situation. However, this is not the same as gritting his teeth and making the best – he has to "learn to love" his lot. I ask: in so far as this is a coherent notion, and meaningfully subject to a decision, is it even something the prisoner *should* decide to attempt?

"Responsible" as a bare adjective

For completeness, there is one last use of "responsible" that I need to mention here, but which I will not be discussing much. Most of this book is concerned with a person being and being held responsible *for* an act or consequences, or *for* another person, or indeed taking responsibility *for* himself or his life. But there are also two inter-related meanings of the adjective "responsible" without any preposition. On the first, when we praise somebody for being "a very responsible young man", we mean a virtuous disposition involving sufficient imaginative awareness of the likely consequences of a tempting but stupid act, and sufficient strength of will to refrain from performing that act despite the temptation. In addition, the responsible young man has demonstrated a willingness to *take* responsibility for the things for which he *is* responsible: if he spills the milk, he will admit it rather than trying to *evade* responsibility. On the second meaning, "responsible" means no more than "competent", in the sense of reaching a threshold of linguistic rationality and understanding appropriate to his age-group and to the situation.[4] The responsible person can understand the age-relevant *practices* of taking responsibility and holding someone responsible, of offering reasons to excuse or justify, of blame and praise for a past act; the responsible person understands enough about human bodies, behaviour and psychology to interact safely with others; and most importantly the responsible person understands enough about conventional definitions of right and wrong, and can reliably recognize the moral quality of their own acts (real or contemplated). As such, animals and young infants are not responsible in this sense, and therefore they are not appropriate targets for reactive attitudes.

FREE WILL, DETERMINISM AND MORAL RESPONSIBILITY

For many philosophers and laypeople alike, the problem of understanding moral responsibility is closely tied up with the problem of free will. And the problem of accommodating human free will in a deterministic universe is one of the largest and oldest problems of philosophy.

There are several different versions of the free will problem. Perhaps the most common frames it in terms of the laws of natural science. Physics, chemistry and biology spend their time trying to describe the bits and bobs that make up the universe, and the way the bits causally interact with the bobs. The guiding assumption throughout is that all these interactions are governed by laws. Scientific progress comprises the gradual discovery of these laws in the sense that the scientists are more and more successful in their predictions about future events. If the chemist discovers that ammonia and matchstick heads can be combined to make a stink bomb (ammonium sulphide), then she can confidently predict that *whenever* ammonia and matchstick heads are introduced, then a foul odour will emerge; indeed, the precise amount of the odour can be predicted once we know the quantities of the inputs. The assumption that all chemical processes are governed by laws (that need to be gradually discovered) entails that the interactions are necessary: given the presence of ammonia and matchstick heads (and the absence of relevant inhibitors), ammonium sulphide *must* be produced. Multiply this simple idea and you get the universe necessarily unfolding in a single, determined direction, governed throughout by the laws.[5]

So here is the problem: if human bodies are part of this determined universe, then they must be equally subject to these causal laws. Although it *feels* as if I am free to cross my right leg over my left, or vice versa, or neither, in fact the interactions between neurons and neurochemicals in my brain have already determined which I shall end up doing. Now, maybe you and I do not know exactly what I shall end up doing, in the same way that we do not know the precise date when the earth shall be engulfed by the swelling sun; but that is a merely epistemic limitation, and does not undermine the fundamental scientific assumption about the complete determinism of the universe.

The problem for moral responsibility begins when we recognize that – under the basic conception of responsibility which I shall be describing in the next chapter – the agent's freedom is a necessary condition for the agent being morally responsible for the act; she had to have been able to do otherwise than what she *chose* to do. In short, if I am to meaningfully blame you for spilling the milk, I have to assume that you were free to take better care when pouring it. If your spilling of the milk was no more than a natural process playing itself out through your limbs, then it would make no more sense to blame you for the spill than it would be to blame a riverbank for bursting.

There are at least two other versions of determinism worth mentioning, and at first glance each of them seems to undermine the possibility of human free will and moral responsibility. If scientific determinism is the first type, then the second, but also most traditional version, requires the presence of an omnipotent omniscient god, who is able to control and predict the future. Everything in the universe is such because God wills it. The normal Christian response to this is to suggest that God deliberately refrains from interfering in human free choice, but this opens up further paradoxes, the most notorious of which is the problem of evil – God can predict that a particular human being will freely choose to cause harm to another, and yet He does nothing to prevent it.

The third form of determinism is psycho-social. Again, as adults we believe we have free will when choosing a career, choosing a mate, choosing where to live, and so on, but in fact we are driven by our characters – the maxim "character is destiny" – which were in turn shaped by our genetic inheritance, our childhood upbringing and chance encounters. It is certain that a good deal of research in the social sciences is based on psycho-social determinism of one degree or another. And there are clear statistical correlations between childhood deprivation or abuse and adult criminality, for example. This form of alleged determinism will be more relevant to what I will be discussing in this book.

I am really not doing justice to what has become an enormously convoluted philosophical discussion. But the nice thing is that I do not need to! Apart from this section, I plan to leave it out of the book altogether. This is partly because it has been treated in excellent detail elsewhere,[6] and I do not have anything to add. But the main reason is that there are still plenty of interesting and relevant problems to fill a philosophical textbook on moral responsibility if we simply *assume* that we have free will.

But there are more reasons than the merely pragmatic. There is a philosophical point here, one that relates to the methodology of the rest of the book. Although the assumption that we have free will is controversial among philosophers, it is not controversial among ordinary people as they go about their ordinary business. This is the point: this book comprises an exploration of the concept of responsibility as spontaneously used by ordinary people in ordinary situations of work, play, family, travel and so on. Some ordinary people, when specifically asked in a philosophy seminar or neuroscience seminar, might flirt with the idea of an entirely deterministic universe. But once they leave the seminar room, then they cannot take the idea seriously.

If we take a frog as a classic example of a biological machine whose movements are based on *no more* than stimulus–response mechanisms (light bounces off fly, into eye, signal processed by brain, tongue shoots out, etc.), then no ordinary person can take seriously the idea that they or other people are remotely like frogs. If I really insisted on seeing other people in ordinary situations as having the metaphysical status of a frog, it is questionable whether I would be able to form any recognizably human relationships with them at all.

In making this assumption, I am supported by two famous philosophical articles, Peter Strawson's 1962 paper "Freedom and Resentment" (reprinted in Strawson 2008) and Harry Frankfurt's 1971 paper "Freedom of the Will and the Concept of a Person" (reprinted in Frankfurt 1988). Strawson argues that in our ordinary interactions, we *cannot help* having reactive attitudes to other people, spontaneous attitudes such as resentment and gratitude, in response to things they do to us. And the very concepts of resentment and gratitude involve holding the agent responsible, which presupposes a sincere belief that the agent acted freely. We may of course come to learn certain facts that force us to revise our initial judgement about their freedom, and the revised judgement might dissolve the reactive attitude. You scowl at me, and I am spontaneously offended; but then I learn that you have a nervous tic which means you scowl at everybody, and my offendedness is undermined. But it is Strawson's point that the default attitude to others is reactive: our first instinct is to take them as being free, and our resentment or gratitude springs up unprompted. This is not to say that determinism is not true; it is merely to say that it can be philosophically legitimate to ignore the problem.

Frankfurt also manages to side-step the free will debate rather than resolve it. Frankfurt examines the attitudes that I can take to my own desires. Here in front of me is a cigarette. I desire to smoke this cigarette. At the same time, I can "look down" on this desire to smoke, as it were from above, and say to myself, "God, I wish I didn't have this craving – cigarettes are expensive, unhealthy and anti-social, I'd love to give it up." And here is Frankfurt's point. If I end up smoking the cigarette, there is a sense that I am being driven by an superficial desire, one that I do not identify with, and so I am not free. If I manage to resist the craving, then I am still acting on a desire, but a deeper one, one that expresses who I am. According to the scientific picture, Frankfurt concedes, *both* desires may still be products of neurochemical influences, and none of us are free. But it still makes sense to say that the reluctant smoker who manages to resist the cigarette is freer than the one who gives in. Sometimes this point is put in terms of the agent's autonomy, precisely in order to distinguish it from the freedom–determinism debate.

OMISSIONS FROM THIS BOOK

So that is it for free will. But even without free will, there are a number of other relevant problems that also have to go if I am to achieve any sort of interesting depth in discussing the main questions. In this section I want to spell out the other topics I will be omitting.

Personal responsibility in the context of democratic politics

The modern state imposes taxes on citizens, and then uses some of the tax revenues to meet the needs of citizens, especially the educational needs, welfare needs (unemployment benefits, incapacity benefits, pensions, etc.) and health needs (in the context of a state-funded health system such as in the UK). In general, a left-winger will favour higher taxes to pay for more redistribution, a right-winger will favour lower taxes and less redistribution. The biggest controversies are in welfare, and sometimes the right-wingers will also invoke the language of personal responsibility as a carrot and a stick:

- Certain citizens have chosen to work hard and to be prudent and thrifty, and in so doing have taken personal responsibility for their lives. The state should reward this responsibility by taxing them less, and this will also act as an incentive for others.

- Certain other citizens have chosen to work less hard, to be less prudent and thrifty, and then rely on the state to bail them out. Citizens should be allowed to suffer the consequences of their irresponsible choices, since this is the only way they will learn. The general message for others would then be not to rely on the largesse of the state to bail them out.

We can frame the disagreement between the right-winger and the left-winger in terms of their differing attitudes to time. The left-winger will examine the citizen's *present* needs, and respond accordingly, regardless of how that person developed these needs, and regardless of the effect any benefit payment will have to encourage or discourage the behaviour of others. The right-winger will judge the present need partly in terms of past choices and future impact, so that their response will be implicitly in terms of praising and blaming the past conduct as "taking" or "avoiding" personal responsibility.

Although I shall not consider these political disputes in this book, there are important philosophical questions I do want to address about the relationship between a person and her past choices. I will also consider some political questions in the area of healthcare (see § "Responsibility for a reckless lifestyle" in Chapter 2). For those who want to pursue the political question in the area of benefits, see the excellent textbooks by Brown (2009), *Personal Responsibility: Why it Matters*, and Matravers (2007), *Responsibility and Justice*.

Collective responsibility

This notion is associated with two events in recent history. The first is the Nazi German occupation of Europe, culminating in the Holocaust, which was planned and carried out by identifiable individuals, but with the collusion, acquiescence or indifference of many more. By now the complex bureaucratic structures of occupation and mass murder have been thoroughly mapped out, and many individuals have been tried and punished for their particular contributions. But there are uncomfortable truths about the different kinds of involvement of mid-level civil servants, soldiers and business managers, as well as of ordinary citizens in both Germany and the rest of Europe. The second major event was the series of financial crises of the past few years, distinguished by the collapse of Enron and the Lehmann Brothers in the US and the debt crises of the peripheral European economies.

There are two relatively unproblematic notions of collective responsibility. Under the concept of legal personhood, companies and states can sign contracts, assume obligations and incur penalties. (And the chief executives of companies can be held responsible in so far as particular ruinous decisions can be traced to them specifically.) Second, any athletic team ultimately wins or loses as a collective, regardless of the contributions of individual players. Otherwise, things are a bit more complicated. It seems to be a basic principle of justice, for example, that only an individual can be punished for the harm he intentionally caused, rather than for his mere membership in a collective. And the idea of holding a collective responsible for the actions of an unknown individual member evokes in many the fiendishly effective but ethically discredited policy of reprisal, which every conqueror, including the Nazis, have used to subdue local populations.

The law can accommodate notions of conspiracy and complicity, but the individual's particular causal contribution to the collective harm has to be robustly demonstrated by the prosecution. In both the Holocaust and the 2008 financial crisis, however, the bureaucratic decision-making was so convoluted, the individual causal contributions so difficult to ascertain, and the collusion so widespread, that it is hard to know where to start when attributing blame.[7] In the financial crisis, there was also the question of government and international regulation in allowing such unbridled greed to affect so many people.

"Continental" responsibility

I hesitate to support the ignorant English-speaking practice of using a single word to encompass philosophers as diverse as Hegel,

Kierkegaard, Sartre, Levinas and Derrida. All of them have written at length on responsibility. However, each of them has their own terminology, their own set of metaphysical assumptions, and their own expectations of the reader, and it would require a great deal of room to do them systematic justice in a textbook such as this. Suffice to say that I am greatly sympathetic to certain "adjectival" ideas, that is, for example, Sartrean or Levinasian ideas, and will be developing them for my own purposes at various points in the text. However, I make no claim to such ideas and their developments being a valid interpretation of the thinkers' texts.

At the very least, one theme that does seem to draw these thinkers together, and which I accept as crucially relevant to any discussion of responsibility, is the presence of the Other. This began as a response to the essential solipsism of Descartes. Descartes *believed* that he lived in a world that was filled with people who looked and behaved much like himself – but he could not be *certain*. He had been deceived by mirages and dreams in the past, and he might be on this occasion; indeed, he was not even certain about the existence of his own body. What he could be certain about, however, was the existence of his own self. This initial philosophical standpoint made, and continues to make, a deep impression on Anglo-American moral philosophers and philosophers of mind, and it continues to drive the huge research into the brain. In moral philosophy, this standpoint begins with essential detachment from the world and from other people, such that an effort then has to be made, and justified, in acting in certain ways towards certain other people.

The above Continental thinkers, roughly speaking, take the existence of the Other to be just as certain as the existence of the Self. The reactive attitudes that Strawson speaks of, the responses that I suggest characterize responsibility, all assume that one of the essential experiences of the world is of a *claim* or *demand* by another (in that world) on my attention, on my thoughts, and on my action. In the context of the spilt milk, the child beholds his scowling mother and there is no doubt in his mind about the reality of the mother and of the demand that her very presence makes on him, whether or not she says anything – one integral part of the encounter with her is the thought that he owes her something, be it an explanation, a denial, an excuse, an apology, something. The child does not ask, as Anglo-American moral philosophers suggest, "What do I have most reason to do?"

Although this example involves a child, the "Continental" idea would see the Other as playing an equally important role in the lives of adults, precisely because the Other's presence has shaped the adult's thought and experience at such a fundamental developmental stage. This does not mean that the self is merely passive in the encounter, and that rational considerations and the will are irrelevant; only that the framework of rational decision-making is more complicated.

Mental illness

The fourth major omission from this book is any sustained discussion of mental illness. There are obvious questions about the degree to which a mentally ill person can be held responsible for an offence, but I simply do not have enough knowledge of psychiatry and psychology, nor do I have enough practical experience of working with mentally ill people to know what mental illness *means* exactly, or what the mentally ill person experiences. In addition, the very category of "mental illness" is huge and ramified, making it difficult to generalize about how responsibility might be affected by different specific illnesses. Lawyers will speak of the individual's lack of "capacity", and in English law will refer to the "M'Naghten rules". These rules were formulated by the House of Lords to justify the acquittal of Daniel M'Naghten in 1843, after he was arrested for murder. The Lords argued that:

> the jurors ought to be told in all cases that every man is to be presumed to be sane, and to possess a sufficient degree of reason to be responsible for his crimes, until the contrary be proved to their satisfaction; and that to establish a defence on the ground of insanity, it must be clearly proved that, at the time of the committing of the act, the party accused was labouring under such a defect of reason, from disease of the mind, as not to know the nature and

quality of the act he was doing; or, if he did know it, that
he did not know he was doing what was wrong.[8]

If the defendant passes either of the tests of insanity, then he can
offer the "insanity defence" to the charge of murder. (Of course,
he might not be deemed to be fit to stand trial in the first place.)
Either way, the result is that the criminal justice system cannot
punish the defendant in the strict sense of the word, but can only
treat him, even if, from the point of view of the defendant, the
method of treatment might in many respects be very similar to
the method of punishment he would have received. For there is a
sound legal principle that the defendant has to understand what he
is being charged with and punished for.

One thing to note about the M'Naghten rules is that they are
purely *cognitive*. That means that they focus on what the defendant
knows or understands about the act. In more recent discussions of
insanity, there is a question of whether the definition of insanity
should be expanded to include a *volitional* criterion. According to
this, the defendant could plead insanity even if he knew full well
the nature and quality of the act and that it was wrong – for he
was driven by an "irresistible impulse". This might be the case with
kleptomania and other well-documented compulsions, especially
when the compelled act involves pointless risks and offers no obvious profit to the actor.

Outside of psychiatry and psychology, philosophers and legal
theorists have contributed to the voluminous literature on mental
illness, but as I say, I do not propose to devote the required space
to this question in this book.[9] I will, however, consider the relationship between responsibility and some milder and more familiar
forms of temporary incapacity, such as intoxication, provocation
or depression.

SOME FINAL NOTES ON METHODOLOGY

This book focuses overwhelmingly on the individual, interacting
with other individuals, in ordinary contexts of family, work and
social spaces. This point about ordinariness is worth expanding.

First, I use a lot of examples. Given that this is a textbook designed for undergraduate philosophy courses, one reason for this is pedagogical: examples focus discussion and restrain some students' eagerness for ungrounded generalization. However, another reason has to do with my long-standing belief that only examples can capture the *particularity* of moral experience. Often I am not confident about the meaning or force of abstract declarations such as "Thou shalt not steal" or even Kant's notorious "Act only according to that maxim by which you can at the same time will that it should become a universal law" (one of the formulations of the "Categorical Imperative"). The most fruitful discussions in moral philosophy, I believe, come from a discussion of whether a person might be justified, say, in stealing in the particular case in which she happens to find herself here and now – and why. Similarly, while it is plausible for Kant to remind us to ask ourselves "What if everyone did that?" before we act, the interesting cases are precisely those where I can be confident that everyone else will *not* do that, and yet I might have good reason to.

Second, my examples and my discussion are drawn from *ordinary situations*. Again, one reason for this is to make the book more accessible to students. But a much bigger reason is because of my suspicion that we cannot learn very much from extraordinary examples precisely because they are extraordinary. Neither I, nor most of the readers of this book, I surmise, have ever experienced anything like the Holocaust, and so it is not at all clear whether I can appeal to their intuitions in trying to make a point based on my own vague intuitions about what I would do in a Holocaust example.[10] In addition, philosophers are fond of using highly fanciful, science fictional or extreme examples, such as those involving runaway trolleys,[11] the dialysis of famous violinists,[12] teletransportation,[13] and being invited to shoot one Indian in order to save nineteen.[14] These examples are deployed to provoke certain simplified intuitions in the reader, and then these intuitions can be used to justify the writer's later controversial philosophical position. I worry, however, that these examples are often so fanciful, and their tone so frivolous about serious matters of life and death, that they cannot provoke *any* reliable intuition except feelings of confusion or disgust. I can honestly say that I have no idea what I would do in the trolley situation. And in so far as a discernible intuition is provoked, I also suggest that such an intuition cannot then be applied to ordinary examples with anything close to the philosophical weight assumed by these writers. The more fanciful the examples get, the more I worry that their author is interested in merely playing a game, scoring points for ingenuity, showing off his command of the fancy tools, rather than being interested in the world or in himself among other people in that world. It has to be said that in opposing these fanciful examples, I am opposing the majority of contemporary Anglo-American moral philosophers. But there is a minority tradition of philosophers (such as Peter Winch and Raimond Gaita) whose influence pervades this book, even when they are not cited explicitly.

Third, let me make a point about the English and American legal cases I have used in this book, especially when discussing excuses. I have to stress that I am not a lawyer and have no formal legal training, so my use of these cases is very much amateur and probably incorrect in many points of interpretative detail; so I will have to beg the knowledgeable reader's forbearance. Nevertheless, as a systematic attempt to articulate moral intuitions surrounding particular cases, I believe that legal cases are immensely useful for any discussion in moral philosophy, but particularly for any discussion of moral responsibility, and I have therefore decided to run the risks of including them.

THE BOOK'S COVER

The striking cover painting is *Orestes Pursued by the Furies*, painted in 1862 by the French painter William-Adolphe Bouguereau. The original story comes from Homer, but was further developed in versions by Aeschylus (*Agamemnon* and *The Libation Bearers*), Sophocles and Euripides, as well as by the twentieth-century American playwright Eugene O'Neill (in his 1931 trilogy *Mourning Becomes Electra*). The great Greek warrior and king Agamemnon was married to Clytemnestra, and they had three children: Iphigenia, Orestes and Electra. At one point in his battles, Agamemnon's fleet was becalmed at sea by the goddess Artemis, and there was a very real risk of mass starvation among his troops and crew if he did not personally sacrifice his beloved Iphigenia to the goddess. With a heavy heart, he proceeded to do this, and the winds picked up again. Upon his return to Greece, he is murdered by Clytemnestra and her lover Aegisthus, partly in revenge for Iphigenia, partly to further Aegisthus's own political ambitions. Orestes and Electra were away at the time of their father's murder, but upon return, Orestes, with Electra's and the god Apollo's encouragement, murdered his mother and her lover in revenge for their father. Immediately after the murder, Orestes is set upon by three Furies (that is the more familiar Latin name: in the Greek they were the Erinyes), underworld deities of justice, for the terrible crime of matricide. Eventually Orestes faces trial before the gods, but is acquitted.

The painting refers to several topics discussed in this book. First and foremost, of course, is the terrible anger in the faces of the Furies, together with the pointing fingers at the stabbed Clytemnestra. Here we have the three elements of the paradigmatic attribution of retrospective moral responsibility: the accuser, the accused, and the grounds of the accusation. Of course, "accuse" is too formal a term, evoking more the slow dignity of the human courtroom than terrifying assaults from supernatural beings. In addition, an accusation might suggest that there remains some doubt about the identity of the offender. In contrast, it is important that the Furies know exactly who did it, that their anger is an unmediated response to the horror of the crime and the depravity of its perpetrator. Most importantly of all, the Furies can be taken as symbolic of the torment of remorse – hence the title of the painting. Even when Orestes believes, and continues to believe, that the murder was justified as an act of revenge, nothing can gainsay the fact not only that his mother was murdered, but that *he did it*. The experience of remorse is the best evidence of the conceptual connection between a crime and the responsibility for that crime.

The story also invokes two other topics in the book. First is distinction between formal legal punishment and personal revenge, however justified the latter act might be. True punishment can only be carried out by the community's authoritative representatives (where "community" refers to any structured group of people, including an institution such as a school or a family). It is only with the trial of Orestes that the cycle of violence can be brought to an end. Second, the story also refers to the prospective responsibility I discuss in Part II. Orestes' deadly mission was motivated by his sense of responsibility to his dead father. He was not merely avenging a death, he was doing what he felt he had to do in his role as Agamemnon's only son (and partly in his role as Electra's brother). And yet Clytemnestra herself could also claim that she did what she had to do out of responsibility to her daughter Iphigenia, just as Agamemnon could also claim that he was responsible above all to his troops and crew.

Above all, however, the painting's central focus is Orestes and his crushing remorse. He does not look at the Furies, let alone attempt to defend or justify himself to them. He is running from the crime, and yet he will never be able to get away from it, even when acquitted by the gods. One of the deepest meanings of responsibility is precisely this radically isolating experience of remorse, which, unlike other kinds of suffering, cannot find solace in companionship, and cannot be healed by time.

1

DEFINING RETROSPECTIVE RESPONSIBILITY

Part I will deal with the backward-looking kind of responsibility for acts in the past. Part II will then examine the forward-looking kind, most associated with roles. Let us recall the paradigmatic situation of the child spilling the milk. The mother enters the room, sees the milk, and instantly knows what happened in the past, and also knows that the child did it. She holds him responsible. And yet this way of phrasing it is ambiguous, for it suggests that she saw the situation and *then* held him responsible. Instead, it would be more accurate to say that she saw his responsibility directly within the situation. Indeed, although the spilling took place in the past, and the spilt milk and overturned cup are here in the present, there is a sense in which the spilling itself is still "in" the spilt milk and overturned cup, here in the present. This might sound odd, so in the first section of this chapter I need to say more about the general notion of the past being in the present, and about what it means for human beings to live in time. This background will turn out to be essential for understanding the nature of retrospective responsibility, which I will then attempt to define in the second section.

THE PAST AND THE PRESENT: TIME, HUMAN LIVES AND AGENCY

It is certainly tempting to think that only the present "really" exists. The past exist*ed*, to be sure, but now it is dead and buried. The past *led* to the present, past events *caused* present states of affairs, some present objects *grew out* of past versions of themselves – that is all clear. But what we have in front of us is the present state of affairs and the present object. We can *infer* facts about the past based on present evidence, as historians and detectives do, we can *reconstruct* what 'must have' happened, but we can never know for sure.

I will call this the "historical" picture, and I will take it to be intuitively plausible among many philosophers and laypeople alike. "We've got to let bygones be bygones", "We mustn't let the past poison the present", "It's all over, you've got to move forward now" – these are familiar expressions, and good advice in any number of situations. On the other hand, I think this picture is not only simplistic, but also leads to some counter-intuitive problems. The most obvious problem is this: why on earth should we *care* about the past if it no longer exists? Why should we *worry* about where we were born and grew up? Why should it matter what Bloggs said or did to me yesterday?

In contrast, I propose a more nuanced account which I will call the "present perfect" account, named after the English tense used in the expression "Have you ever worked in high finance?" This is to be distinguished from the simple present ("Are you working in high finance?") because the work took place in the past. But more interestingly, it is also to be distinguished from the simple past ("Did you work in high finance during the boom years?"), where the enquiry has to do with placing the event in a sequence of remembered personal and geopolitical events, with more or less clear causal relations between events. Despite the misleading content of the enquiry, the present perfect is very much a present tense. It asks: how are you now different because of your work in high finance during the boom years? Indeed, the present perfect is not necessarily interested in when exactly you worked in high finance, merely that it is an experience which might have shaped your thoughts, shaped your character, and shaped your understanding of the world. My question implies my belief that the experience is still "in" you in this way.

22

There is an ambiguity about this "in". The historical account has plenty of room for experiential *memories* in you, as one kind of evidence of the past among others. But when I ask you whether you have worked in high finance, I am not asking you to consult your memory as you would your diaries from that period; I am asking something about *you*, here and now, and how you think you might have been changed in a deeper way than merely acquiring new memories. Are you now wealthy as a result of your work? Do you understand better than the rest of us the background to the political stories in the newspapers? And most pointedly of all: do you feel any shame or responsibility now about your direct involvement with a culture that led to the ruin of so many people?

Of course I accept that there are situations and contexts when one has to move on from the past. But here is my point: the very advice to you to move on presupposes that the past still has a grip on you. This grip is more than a mere memory or a reminiscence, it suggests unfinished business lingering into the present. The wound I see in your flesh before me does not lead me to *infer* a past stabbing. Your grief does not lead me to make a *reasonable guess* that someone close to you has recently died – I can see the stabbing in the wound, and I can see your friend's death in your face. I want to say that the stabbing and the wound are *conceptually* (non-accidentally) linked: in thinking about the latter, I am also thinking directly about the former.

I am not saying that the past still exists somewhere or "somewhen". Rather, it is a mistake to think of the present as logically separate from the past such that, in principle, *anything* could have happened five minutes ago and we could only make a better or worse guess on the basis of fallible rules of evidence. According to the historical account, there is no real objection to the radically sceptical possibility that the universe came into being five minutes ago, together with all our false memories of what happened before then. My present perfect account must reject that possibility as inconceivable, given how much we are invested in the past, and how much of our lives we live out through the past, into the present, and indeed into the future.

The idea of conceptual links between the present and the past is also important for our understanding of human beings. Part of our understanding of what a human being is, here and now, is that he has led a life through to the present moment. At the very least, he is "from" somewhere, speaks a particular language, has family and friends somewhere in the world, such that his relationships with those family and friends and with that place necessarily stretch far back from the present. In short: he has a story, a story that can in principle be told about how he got from there to here, from then to now. Even when the individual's physical and mental characteristics change through time, for example between the ages of five and twenty-five, it still makes sense to say that the earlier and later individuals are merely different stages of the *same* person, tracing a single path through space and time.

There is a second-order aspect to this identity through time. Just as an individual human being develops through time, so too do his relationships with certain family members and friends. Each relationship has a beginning, a progression, certain defining events, a story. In the same way that the individual's past is in his present, the relationship's past is in its present. Think of how an act of betrayal, if it does not end the relationship, will inevitably colour the subsequent course of it.

I have been stressing the temporal aspect of our understanding of other human beings. There is another aspect that has been much more central to philosophical enquiry, and that is the aspect of agency. Human beings not only experience the world, they act in it: they hit things, push things, launch things, create things, but they also say things and write things, all of which disrupt the natural course of events. And more importantly, they tend to act for *reasons*. Sometimes the reasons for an individual's action will be obvious to an observer; sometimes the agent will have to give his reasons in order to make his action intelligible. The agent's and the observer's sensitivity to reasons also works across time. When we meet another human, we do not simply wonder what has happened to him but also what he has done, and – if not immediately obvious – why he has done it. We assume that the agent can in principle give an explanation or an account: in that sense the default attitude of one human being to another is to assume *accountability*, a word that is normally used in institutional-hierarchical relations, but is wider in its basic meaning. For reasons to work as reasons in making present or past actions intelligible, a great many understandings have to be shared among individual human beings, understandings about why people do things. There is still room for disagreement about the "real" reason, about whether the reason was a "good" one or not for performing a certain action, and there is plenty of room for stubborn bafflement despite one's best imaginative and sympathetic efforts; but these are exceptions to the general assumption of mutual intelligibility guiding all our relationships past and present.

THE BLAME GAME

It is against this background – the lingering past and mutual human intelligibility – that the "blame game" between accuser and accused makes sense. I am deliberately using the term "game" to emphasize two thoughts: that the practice of blaming is governed by rules, and that the rules govern both people's involvement. In this section we shall examine the game more closely, using a classic example from our favourite Whodunnit. The body of Miss Scarlett lies in the drawing room with a knife in her back, and Miss Marple is on the case. She interviews witnesses, she gathers evidence and murder weapons and alibis, she charts movements and eliminates suspects, she discovers motives, and ultimately points the finger at … Colonel Mustard. So far, she is doing no more than seeking the cause, and the finger pointing involves holding Mustard causally responsible. It is only when Mustard is duly arrested, formally charged, and confesses to the crime that questions of moral responsibility begin. After all, Mustard might say no more than that he did not and could not have done it, and he might be able to introduce more evidence and testimony of which Miss Marple was unaware. But Mustard confesses, and the blame game begins. The first step is the accusation. The second step is the defendant's response. The third step is the court's assessment of this response, and a final decision about the defendant's responsibility. The fourth step is the punishment.

There is a question here about the difference between moral responsibility and *legal* or *criminal liability*, but I am going to ignore this for now – the legal context is useful to examine, precisely because of its highly formalized nature. But the blame game takes place in all manner of informal contexts as well, from children spilling milk to football teams losing to adults divorcing; it is an essential part of both casual and intimate human relationships. Indeed, as Garrath Williams persuasively argues (2013), we first learn the concept of responsibility and blame within the context of the family and of early friendships: the practice of one person holding another responsible takes place against a background of two people who already *share* responsibility for one another's lives, thus giving one the "standing" to blame the other. In contrast, blame by a non-friend or non-family-member can be more easily deflected as "none of their business".

Behind the accusation against Mustard are three crucial assumptions, and Mustard's response may then involve showing that at least one of these assumptions is false, and therefore that he is not, or not fully, morally responsible, even if he remains causally responsible. These three assumptions are the Capacity assumption, the Understanding assumption and the Control assumption.[1]

The Capacity assumption

In order to take part in the blame game, the defendant needs to have sufficient mental capacity to understand the accusation and the possibility that it might be inaccurate or incomplete in relation to his own memories, to understand the nature and quality of the act he is accused of committing in the past, and to understand his options in terms of available defences. In addition, if he is to be condemned and punished, he has to be able to understand the punishment *as* punishment *for* the crime which *he* committed; without such an understanding, he will not experience the criminal justice procedure or the punishment as anything other than arbitrary power.

There are two main categories of defendants lacking capacity – the mentally ill and children. I have already said in the Introduction that I would not discuss the mentally ill (and the "insanity defence"). I will have more to say about children, but clearly a child can reasonably be held morally responsible under blame game rules for offences of increasing severity as he or she ages. A five-year-old should be able to understand and learn from Mum's terrible scowl. At what age a child can understand the particular evil of murder is a controversial question. In one notorious case involving the murder of the English toddler James Bulger in 1993, the two perpetrators were considered sufficiently mature to be held morally and criminally responsible at the age of ten years. Most jurisdictions seem to place it at twelve or fourteen years. Anyway, for the moment I am talking about an adult of sound mind named Colonel Mustard in developing a paradigm case.

The Understanding assumption

In accusing Mustard of murder, the judge is assuming that Mustard understood enough about the situation and about what he was doing in response to that situation. More specifically, the accusation assumes that the *best* description, from Mustard's own perspective, of the act he was intending to carry out was "murder". The Understanding assumption overlaps with the Capacity assumption because the defendant needs to understand a lot about death and pointed objects and the vulnerable spots on the human body in order to commit murder; and he needs to understand that murder is a bad thing. But Mustard can also be assumed to understand that the person whom he was killing was indeed Miss Scarlett, and not someone else.

The Understanding assumption forms the basis of a first class of "defences" against the accusation; that is, the accusation is made, and then the defendant can explain that, in fact, he did not realize what he was doing, or if he did realize it, he did not understand it was wrong. We will examine the nature of defences, below.

The Control assumption

Mustard is assumed to have had the power and freedom, and to know he had the power and freedom, to perform or refrain from performing the act in question. Mustard was therefore in *control* of the act. In fact the Control condition could be construed in a way that would include the Understanding assumption: for it is only when I understand what I am doing that I can be said to fully control it. However, it will be clearer for my purposes to keep the two conditions apart. Once again, denying the Control assumption is the basis for a number of different defences against the accusation: one can say that one was "forced" to do the action, for example.[2]

DEFENCES

Before we go on, I want to again stress how *ordinary* all this is in non-detective-novel situations. As observers, we make causal and moral responsibility attributions all the time, without thinking. It is very rare that we stop to dwell on the three assumptions – usually it takes a mere glance at the situation to accept that such-and-such a person is morally responsible. And for society and relationships to work with any sort of complexity, these common and finely tuned responsibility attributions have to work quickly and reliably. As children we learn the rules of the blame game, slowly and painfully, every time we spill the milk or thump our little brother. It is only against this background obviousness that more complicated cases and problems can even make sense, let alone be resolved.

In the same way as accusations are very ordinary, so too are defences. "Defences" is a legal word, and it comprises anything that can be said in one's favour as a *response* to the accusation. The two main categories of defences are excuses and justifications. The most common defence is the excuse of the honest mistake. This is perhaps less easy to imagine in the case of a fatal stabbing, so consider instead the crowded tram. The tram lurches, and I collide with my neighbour. "I'm so sorry, I didn't mean to", I say quickly. This involves an acknowledgement of causal responsibility for the discomfort that my neighbour suffered, but a denial of moral responsibility or blameworthiness, for I did not have the intention to harm him, did not know that the tram would lurch just at that moment, and I had taken reasonable precautions against the known risk that the tram would lurch. Or imagine an ordinary justification: I am engrossed in something, and do not notice a mosquito landing on my arm and beginning to suck. You come over and swat my arm. I look up, astounded at this gratuitous act of sadism; you point at the dead mosquito and flick it off. Instantly my indignation disappears and is replaced by mild gratitude. What seemed cruel turned out to be kind. And here is the thing: most of the time, that expression of an excuse or justification is enough to resolve the matter, and both parties move on in their lives. Too much attention at the law courts and philosophy seminars can blind one to this essential ordinariness!

Let us now distinguish between an excuse and a justification more systematically. Both can be offered to deflect blame, in part or in whole, while accepting causal responsibility for an act. But the deflection is fundamentally different in form. Sometimes these two categories will overlap; sometimes the same words uttered by the agent can function as either or both an excuse and a justification. The trick is to distinguish them by examining the intention, or inferring the intention by looking at the evidence before and after the act.

Excuses

An *excuse* acknowledges that the act was indeed harmful,[3] but shows that the agent was not morally responsible for the resulting harm. An excuse therefore comprises a separation of the agent from the act. The harmful consequences were generated through the agent's body, as it were, but the origin of the act was outside the agent's self, without enough of the agent's control or understanding. I say "self" rather than "body": the disruption of brain function that characterizes an epileptic fit is inside the body, but still outside the self. If I damage your property during the fit, I have an excuse because my body was being "driven". Again, excuses will depend heavily on normative standards of what a person can be reasonably expected to understand or control. If the agent did not understand what he should have understood, or if he did not have as much control as he should have had in that situation, then he may be guilty of recklessness or negligence – and therefore morally responsible for the harm done. More on this ere long.

The sheer variety of excuses is a lot greater than we often realize. In addition to my ignorance of the tram's imminent lurch, we can imagine many situations where we might be tempted to proffer an excuse. Whether or not any of the following (non-exhaustive) list of examples could generate an excuse that would actually be accepted formally or informally is another question: some of the proffered excuses might be met with counter-accusations of recklessness or negligence. But this is the point about the blame game, that an excuse is merely the next step, without necessarily being the final step.

- *Ignorance of unfamiliar rules.* I am visiting a foreign city. Although I purchase a tram ticket from the machine, I fail to understand that it must be date-stamped to be valid.
- *Unpredicted effects.* I washed the tile floor, and before it dried the telephone rang, you came running out of your room and slipped on the floor.
- *Underestimated risk.* I go camping with your tent. Because it is raining, I light the gas stove inside the tent's awning, and the tent catches fire.
- *Distraction.* I am driving. I am also thinking of the pleasant romantic encounter from the night before. I crash into the car in front of me.
- *Foot in mouth syndrome.* My friend Bloggs describes a merry evening in the pub last night. When I later meet his wife, I mention my encounter with Bloggs, and the merry evening. It turns out that he had told her he was staying late in the office.[4]

Whether or not a proffered excuse is accepted will depend on standards of reasonable behaviour, which itself will depend on standards of reasonable perception, deliberation and emotional reaction. These standards have to be learned by children by imitating competent standard-followers and by accepting authoritative correction of their own self-serving attempts to avoid responsibility. If the child promises to tidy his room, and then ignores his promise because he remembers that there is something good on the telly, it will be explained to him that this is not a good excuse.

There may of course be some disagreement between two individuals in certain cases about whether a given excuse is reasonable or not; but the existence of occasional disagreement should not be taken as evidence that these standards are non-existent, arbitrary or mere expressions of power. A society and its legal system can only hold itself together because the vast majority *agree* on what constitutes a reasonably good excuse in a particular situation, and agree on paradigm cases of good and bad excuses in the shared stories that partly comprise popular culture (including the stories involving the upbringing of children). They will also agree on certain more lenient standards for certain classes of agent, for instance tourists. In addition, we can often presuppose a basic good will on crowded trams to allow apologies for honest ignorance to be promptly offered and accepted among strangers in a way that quashes spontaneous resentment and lubricates the inevitable frictions of crowded public space.

Justification

To reiterate, a successful excuse removes the agent's moral responsibility, while leaving the act morally unchanged. A *justification* begins with the acceptance of the accuser's assumptions of capacity, understanding and control, and acknowledges that the act was *prima facie* wrong, but provides additional detail, a "bigger picture". For example, the harmful act was reasonably judged to be necessary to prevent a much greater harm, as when a stranger violently pushes me out of the way of an oncoming truck. The stranger's intention was not to push me ("small picture") but to push-me-out-of-the-way of the truck ("big picture"). We then say that the harm was justified, and that the act – "all things considered" – turns out not to be a morally bad act, and therefore there is no longer anything to blame the agent for. Consider the following examples:

- lying out of kindness ("No, your bum looks fine in that");
- an ambulance going through a red light;

31

- self-defence, in the case where the aggressor presents a credible, severe and imminent threat to the person or to someone close to him, and the defensive force must be a last resort and proportionate to the threat (for discussion of six different kinds of self-defence, see Thomson 1991);
- two men are hiking, far from civilization, when they are caught in a sudden heavy snowstorm. They break into an empty cottage, light a fire, eat the food, and decide to wait for help there (sometimes this trespass and theft is justified by what the law calls "necessity").

The point about the "small picture" and the "big picture" has to do with the possible descriptions of the action. Any action will be subject to a number of different descriptions, and often the most interesting is that under which the agent was acting. In the self-defence example, the agent's intention is not merely to kill, but to disable or deter the aggressor *by* killing. If he knew how to disable or deter the aggressor by any other, less lethal, means, then he would have certainly preferred to have done so. If his justification is recognized by the court, he will be acquitted. It is still the case that he *killed* another person, but there is no longer the suggestion that he *murdered* him; for murder by definition involves the big-picture intention to murder, not the small-picture intention to kill as the only recognizable means of carrying out the big-picture intention of saving one's life. Of course, even if the court acquits the protagonist of murder, it still remains a fact that he knowingly caused another person's death. However much he reminds himself of his legal and moral innocence, there is a powerful sense in which he will not be the same again. I will return to this theme in Chapter 5 on moral luck.

Excuses vs. justification

A threat to one's life, either from a human aggressor or from an emergency situation, could also be classed as an excuse. Rather than coolly weighing up reasons for and against, the protagonist might have been driven by panic or fear. If my act of self-defence were a *gut reaction* to the threat, it would be as if the situation had overwhelmed my capacity to think and intend. If I were hungry and weak and delirious after three days of walking in a snow-storm, I might have broken into the house out of sheer despera-tion. However, in the legal context, the difference might not be too important, since the court could accept either as grounds for with-holding blame.

A more complicated case of ambiguity between excuse and jus-tification would be the following. A woman suffers from systematic domestic abuse by her husband over many years. One day she buys a can of petrol. Once her husband falls asleep, she pours the petrol on him, and sets him alight, killing him. Can she defend herself by recourse to an excuse or a justification (or neither)?[5] Clearly this is not a normal case of provocation or self-defence, since the husband was asleep and not in a position to provoke anyone in the moments leading up to his death; nor was it a panicky response in the heat of the moment, for she had planned and prepared the kill-ing during the previous day or days.

Now, the defence counsel could claim "diminished responsibil-ity" by proffering the *excuse* based on the destabilization of the woman's mental faculties by the years of abuse. In other words, the counsel would be arguing that she was driven to do it by the abuse, and that she herself had become incompetent in the proc-ess. On the other hand, the defence counsel could also claim that the killing was *justified* by her reasonable fear of future abuse, by her fear for her children suffering similar abuse, and by her belief that she would always be recaptured and punished after further escape attempts. In arguing for an excuse of diminished responsi-bility, the defence counsel would be essentially saying the woman lacked full capacity; this has the drawback of not doing enough to recognize the injustice that she has suffered, or to recognize her right to defend herself from a severe, credible, although not imme-diate threat; indeed, the excuse does not seem to offer the woman sufficient respect as a person forced to choose the lesser evil.[6]

I will return to a more standard example of provocation, below. Before that, however, I need to make a quick aside about the phe-nomenon of value pluralism, and the opportunity of the court to take, or not to take, this into account in its evaluation of defences.

VALUE PLURALISM

I want to introduce a point here, one that will return at several places in the book. The phrase "value pluralism" has become rather fashionable in these days of liberal multicultural societies. The thought is that, in the political sphere, different people have different values and these differences ought to be respected. The accompanying thought, also prompted by interminable ethical debates about euthanasia and abortion in the press and in philosophy seminars, is that there are no "absolute" values, and that morality is entirely subjective, like one's taste in music or in clothing.

I do not want to enter the political debate about multiculturalism. But I do want to take a forceful stand against ethical subjectivism. Not only is it utterly untrue to the lives that we lead, it is also dangerously frivolous. It is untrue because all of us live lives in which we cannot help taking ethical concepts such as justice, generosity, promises, betrayal and murder seriously; if someone *genuinely* believed that all values were merely subjective, then, for a start, he would not have any friends. For friendship requires loyalty, and that means occasionally going against one's self-interest purely for the sake of the friend's well-being; and that is an ethical stance that is required by the very definition of friendship. It is perfectly possible to cultivate an attitude of mere investment towards another person – short-term sacrifice in exchange for a long-term return on the investment – but such a person will not be a friend. Ethical subjectivism is also dangerously frivolous, because it is often used as an excuse for cowardly inaction in the face of injustice and evil.

More pertinent to our discussion, subjectivism can also be squarely rejected when we consider the fact that we share human bodies with the same vulnerabilities to illness, injury, hunger and death. The two examples of justification above – self-defence and necessary trespass – both rely on our immediate and imaginative understanding of the sort of threat to life and health that the two situations present. When it comes to serious threats, there is no value pluralism. In both cases of self-defence and necessary trespass there will of course be questions about fuzzy borders: how much of a credible threat justifies a response in the form of an intentional attempt to kill? How much of a perceived survival risk justifies the trespass? And some might argue that the fuzziness of the border undermines the confident rejection of ethical subjectivism. But consider the fuzzy boundaries of more ordinary concepts such as chairs. Is a stool a chair? Is a bench? Maybe it is, maybe it is not – but that does not mean that I cannot reliably use the concept "chair" to identify paradigm examples.

However, value pluralism can be a factor in the case of less serious situations, and this can affect the question of whether one is responsible or not, and to what degree. Do I conceal my colleague's laziness from our superiors? A lot will depend on the situation, of course, but even with all the particulars spelled out, different people may well respond to this dilemma in different ways, in accordance with the different values that inform their response – even if we could not fault any of them individually for a hasty or superficial judgement. However, it is important to understand two aspects of this plurality. First, it always exists within limits, beyond which everybody can be presumed to share the same relevant values. If the colleague is lazy to the point of not turning up to work without a good reason for absence (e.g. serious illness), then I have no reason to cover for him; if his laziness in our engineering firm endangers public safety, then I have a positive duty to inform my superiors about the situation. Second, even within those limits, when you and I disagree about the ethically best course of action, this is not a mere *preference* – we can still adduce reasons in favour of our position, each in an attempt to persuade the other, and these reasons will themselves be subject to shared standards of what constitutes good reasons. This should be contrasted with something that is genuinely subjective, such as one's taste in clothing or music, where there will often come a point where no further reasons can be given for simply liking something.

This constrained value pluralism, then, leads to a deeply ramified question for institutional attributions of responsibility and the evaluation of proffered defences: should the institution favour a more *objective* approach or a more *subjective* approach? The objective approach focuses on some notion of shared values and standards, and is typically invoked by asking what an idealized "reasonable person" would or would not do in such a situation. The subjective approach focuses on what the actual defendant – as far as we can tell about her character – genuinely believed or wanted in the given situation. If the institutional approach is too objective, this risks being unfair on certain defendants who fall far short of any general shared standards comprising the reasonable person; if the institutional approach is too subjective, then there is a real risk of losing any standards against which to hold them responsible, since everyone "does their best", of course.

In the next two sections of this chapter, I would like to examine two important defences, both of which generate issues of more objective or subjective approaches taken by the court. Both of them relate to the Control assumption behind attributions of responsibility; that is, both involve deflecting the accusation by saying that, in fact, the defendant did not have as much control over his actions as the accuser assumes. *Prima facie*, the defendant seems responsible – the onus to explain the defence is very much on the defendant. So the question here concerns the sort of things that the defendant can say as a valid defence, and the sort of things that will be relevant when the court evaluates the defences within the particular circumstances as it understands them.

DURESS AND COERCION

A paradigmatic case here involves an armed robber who enters a small shop and demands the solitary cashier to give him the contents of the cash register. With or without speaking, a credible threat to life and health is presented by the gun, and the cashier understands the threat. The cashier complies, and thereby knowingly assists the theft of the shop's money (she is only an employee of the shop's owner). However, when accused of being an accessory to a crime, she offers the defence of duress. This could be an excuse or a justification. As a justification, the cashier argues that her compliance was only *prima facie* wrong. In the "big picture" which includes the credible threat, the compliance option turns out to be the least worst, and therefore the morally justifiable, option for her. In this case the act itself is morally and legally permissible. (Note that I am speaking only about the act of the cashier's compliance;

the robber remains guilty whatever the verdict on the cashier, of course.) No reasonable person could ask her to undergo a great risk to her life and health to safeguard her employer's property, and so it makes sense to say that she was "forced". But she might offer duress as an excuse, in the sense that the situation so overwhelmed her that she instinctively handed over the cash, and therefore her act could not be considered sufficiently voluntary (under her control) for a valid attribution of moral responsibility.

So let us consider the "objective" approach and the "subjective" approach that could be adopted in this paradigm case. The objective approach relies on what a person of "reasonable firmness" would withstand before giving in to the threat in that situation. Part of the situation is the particular nature of the threat: if the bank robber came in with a bucket of water and threatened to throw it at the cashier, then she could be reasonably expected to resist. Another part would be the options available for avoiding the threat: if there were an armed security guard present, if there were a back door she could run out of (and if she could be reasonably expected to *know* about the security guard or back door), and so on. A third part of the situation that might be relevant would be the cashier's physical physique – if she were a burly army sergeant, then she could be reasonably expected to resist threats of unarmed physical violence better than a person of average stature and background, for example. Notice here that we are talking about the *cashier*, and yet we are including her burly physique in the *situation*. And as such we are still taking an objective approach by asking what a reasonable member of that class would do in such a type of situation.

Contrast this with a "subjective" approach, which considers the particular identity of this cashier, that is, her particular commitments and values that might make her vulnerable in a particular way. Imagine if our cashier, in her spare time, is passionate about orchids: she cultivates them on a discreet allotment, sells them, sells photographs of them, enters them in competitions, and so on. (Notice that she does not simply declare to the court that she cares about orchids; she reveals her care by her extended demonstrable emotional involvement with them.) While she is tending the shop, the robber comes in, not with a gun, but with a menacing smile, and says: "I know where your orchids are. Better cough up." It is not her life or health that is under threat here, but her orchids; but the credible threat to her orchids distresses her immensely, and she complies with the robber's demands. The shop-owner is irate: "You handed over all my money for the sake of some bloody flowers? I'll make sure you pay for this!"

In fact, this "subjective" approach to duress is both objective and subjective. The approach accepts that human beings in general have intelligible commitments and values which make them vulnerable to pressure. In the case of the robber's direct threat to life and health, then the assumption is that the cashier *cares* about her life and health, and therefore her compliance is justifiable. In looking more closely at an idiosyncratic care such as the cashier's for her orchids, the approach is objective in form but subjective in content. However, it should be noticed that not *anything* can be intelligibly cared about. If the cashier tried to justify her compliance with the robber on the grounds of a threat to her toenail collection, the court would have serious grounds for doubting her sanity. I chose orchids because they seem to lie on a boundary: on the one hand, they are indeed just "bloody flowers", on the other hand they are things of great beauty that do inspire serious passion in a not negligible minority of enthusiasts. There is a case for saying that life and health is a more fundamental value here, precisely because it can be taken as equally and deeply valued by all human beings, and because one needs life and health in order to *then* appreciate anything else such as orchids. But whether one can derive a plausible hierarchy of values here, the fact remains that in the particular situation of the second robbery, it is the cashier's beloved orchids that are credibly threatened, while she was not worried about her life and health.

So the risks of taking a more subjectivist account of duress should be evident. However, there are problems with taking a purely objectivist account as well. Consider a third version of the shop example. This time the cashier hates her employer, and has been waiting for an opportunity to get revenge after being passed over in promotion. At the same time, this cashier is an expert in handguns: she owns four of them, she reads the magazines, she regularly visits shooting ranges. In comes a robber who waves a gun in her face, and demands money. Now, this gun is in fact made of plastic, but a non-expert would take the threat as credible. Our cashier, however, notices the fake right away. But seizing the opportunity, she pretends to sob and plead "Please don't shoot me!", and starts eagerly handing over the cash. The robber fills his bag, turns to go, and for good measure, she adds "I'm so scared, I'm so scared" for the benefit of the CCTV. A purely objectivist account would recognize her defence and deem her not responsible for assisting the theft.

One way out of this would be to take the agent's skills and expertise as components of the objective situation. In the same way that the agent's burly army sergeant physique is relevant to the firmness that we can reasonably expect of her in response to physical threats, so too we can take her fire-arms expertise and her military experience in hand-to-hand combat to be relevant. This is interesting because the expertise and the experience are both "in" the agent, and yet we are attributing them to the situation external to the agent. In a similar way, we can also take into account the agent's diagnosed psychological impediments to action – phobias and compulsions – as supporting a duress defence. If the robber knew that the cashier was a severe claustrophobic (and this could be corroborated in court by authoritative medical testimony), then he could threaten to lock her in a closet unless she revealed the code to the safe. Chances are, the duress defence would be recognized since the phobia would be understood as an external factor limiting her will in the same way as the credible threat of physical pain would limit the non-phobic person.[7]

PROVOCATION

In this section I want to consider the defence of provocation. The classic case here is the man who kills his wife upon finding her *in flagrante* with another man. On the face of it, it looks like an intentional act of murder, albeit without planning or malice aforethought. Behind the accusation, once again, lie the three assumptions of capacity, understanding and control. The defence of provocation is most easily understood as an excuse based on the rejection of the Control assumption: the red mist descended over the defendant and he could not do otherwise than what he did. Importantly, however, provocation should be distinguished from something like an epileptic fit. If an epileptic causes damage to a friend's Ming vase during a fit, there is a real sense that it was not *him* who did the damage, but *his body*, which had been effectively hijacked. His defence against the accusation of wilful damage would be to reject the Capacity assumption. When the husband is provoked, he does not collapse in a helpless heap; quite the contrary, his mind and instrumental reasoning is terrifyingly focused on the tools and tactics for carrying out the murderous task – he fetches a kitchen knife and not a tennis ball, he strikes his wife in the middle of the back and not in her leg, and so on.

Provocation involves the "diminishment" of the responsibility rather than the elimination of it. Typically provocation is only invoked as a defence to the charge of murder; and if successful the charge will be reduced from murder to manslaughter – and the defendant still goes to prison. So there is a residual thought that he could have and should have controlled his understandable impulses. No matter how painful the adultery is, it is nowhere near as serious as murder.

There is some confusion in the English law at present. For many years, sexual infidelity had been recognized as sufficient grounds for the defence of provocation and the diminishment of responsibility. However, there have also been long-standing arguments that such a recognition came too close to allowing overly jealous husbands to kill their wives when they merely suspected infidelity. As a result, the Coroners and Justice Act 2009[8] declared that sexual infidelity would no longer ground the defence of provocation. However, the recent case of *R* v. *Clinton (Jon-Jacques)* [2012][9] has cast doubt on this. Clinton, the husband, was recognized as having been provoked into killing his wife, although the provocative actions constituted not only the wife's sexual infidelity but also her sexual mockery and humiliation of Clinton. Despite the confusion in the law, I am going to be taking the jealous husband situation as paradigmatic for my discussion.

There is a larger question here concerning how responsible we are for our emotions. The adultery example might support a widespread but false understanding of the emotions as: (a) primarily things which just wash over one randomly, unpredictably, and which are experienced in a purely passive way, in the same way that one would experience a hangover; (b) primarily things that *distort* perception and deliberation, so that anything done under the influence of emotion is necessarily non-autonomous. In response, it is true that sometimes emotions do wash over one unexpectedly, and can sometimes distort one's autonomous wishes. But most of the time, emotions are just the opposite. First, emotions are responses to specific situations, and are subject to standards of appropriateness. When I discover that I have been betrayed, I am supposed to get angry; when I discover that I have done something morally wrong, I am supposed to feel remorseful. Second, emotions are ways of seeing and thinking: love for someone makes me particularly attentive to aspects of her being that would elude the dispassionate observer; that I feel remorse for what I have done means that I have fully understood how wrong and hurtful it was – lack of appropriate emotional response can sometimes reveal a lack of appropriate understanding.

The husband's killing of the adulterous wife is complicated by the ambiguous status of the emotion of jealousy. With a view to the previous paragraph, we could say that the appropriateness of his jealousy is what supports the interpretation of diminished responsibility. But *can* jealousy be justified? Perhaps people from different parts of Europe will answer this question in different ways. As a "Northern European", I am inclined to see jealousy as a sign of immaturity, possessiveness and insecurity: a healthy relationship is characterized by the trust and respect that would allow the partner her freedom. Jealousy would still be a natural response to suspected infidelity, but the agent would and should try, as best he can, to ignore it as an illegitimate voice in his deliberations, in the same way as he would try to ignore pangs of hunger or lust at inopportune times. In contrast, a "Southern European" would see jealousy as evidence of a genuine passionate love that the cold fish of the north are incapable of achieving. One of the consequences of love is that it makes the lover vulnerable: to insist otherwise is to be stuck in a solipsistic and instrumental understanding of intimate relationships. Jealousy might be debilitating and humiliating, but the risk of jealousy directly flows from opening oneself to the other so completely.

One test to determine whether to accept or reject the provocation defence would be to ascertain the defendant's attitude to the murder after the red mist has past. Lingering vindictiveness would suggest deeper culpability, perhaps going back years, whereas horrified remorse would incline one to the view that the defendant was genuinely "not himself" in committing the act. But such a test is difficult since presumably every defendant on trial for murder has little to lose in acting out the role proposed by his defence counsel.

As with duress, there is a problem of whether to take a more objective or a more subjective approach to provocation. Should we allow the defence only in situations where we believe the "reasonable person" would also have been provoked to murder? Or should we try our best to take the defendant as he was: seek out testimony and evidence for his background and character traits in order to imagine roughly what *he* could be reasonably expected to resist? Both approaches face the risk of unfairness in different ways, either by letting not enough people or too many people off the hook. Throughout, the court has to push for a standard of proof beyond reasonable doubt; even though many criminals thereby avoid punishment, at least the number of falsely punished is minimized.

CONCLUSION

Throughout this chapter, we have been describing certain aspects of the "blame game". This term is useful because it invokes a set of shared rules that govern the game, and because it emphasizes that there are at least two people in the game, the accuser and the accused, and that they are having a conversation. Hence questions of attributing moral responsibility begin with the accusation, but then wait upon the defendant to take the next turn in the game. Often the truth of the matter can only be converged upon through this conversation, with both sides seeking support from evidence and testimony. Although this book is a work of *moral* philosophy, I have been drawing much of the discussion from *legal* contexts, on the assumption that the blame game of the latter is a usefully formalized version of the blame game in the former. Later in the book, I will be taking greater care to distinguish the moral from the legal.

One of the responses available to the defendant is that he did not *intend* the act in question. This usually reduces the degree of his responsibility for the harm caused, although it may not eliminate it. However, there is a lot more to be said about responsibility for unintended acts and consequences, and to that we now turn.

2

RESPONSIBILITY FOR MISTAKES

The previous chapter mostly concerned the problem of attributing moral responsibility, within the context of the "blame game", to individuals for their *intentional* actions. Even when the individual offered further details about himself or about the situation, details designed to excuse him in part or in full and thereby diminish his responsibility, the act in question remained intentional. I also mentioned in passing another category of excuse, and that was the *unintentional* mistake or accident – that is what this chapter is about. The kind of mistakes and accidents I will be focusing on involve unambiguous causal responsibility for the harmful or expensive or embarrassing consequences, but a denial of full moral responsibility: "Yes, I broke your vase, but I didn't mean to." What does this statement mean, exactly, and what sort of residual responsibility do I retain?

AUSTIN'S DONKEY

We have to start by distinguishing mistakes and accidents, and the best thing is to draw from J. L. Austin's famous example:

> You have a donkey, so have I, and they graze in the same field. The day comes when I conceive a dislike for mine. I

go to shoot it, draw a bead on it, fire: the brute falls in its tracks. I inspect the victim, and find to my horror that it is *your* donkey. I appear on your doorstep with the remains and say – what? "I say, old sport, I'm awfully sorry, &c., I've shot your donkey *by accident*"? Or "*by mistake*"? Then again, I go to shoot my donkey as before, draw a bead on it, fire – but as I do so the beasts move, and to my horror yours falls. Again the scene on the doorstep – what do I say? "By mistake"? Or "by accident"? (Austin 1956: 29 n. 4)

In the first case, I misperceived – *mis-took* – the situation, I thought that your donkey was actually mine. The important point is that I could in principle have avoided the mistake by getting a better look at the two donkeys, that is, it was in my power to be more careful about what I was aiming at. Even if I thought at the time that I had correctly identified my donkey and it did not occur to me that I needed to look closer, there is an important sense in which, later, I will say "I should have looked closer". In the second case, I had correctly identified my donkey, and it was not in my power to prevent it moving at the last moment; it was an accident that "befell" me.

The response from the neighbour will then be different depending on whether it was a mistake or an accident, and this response will correspond to the degree of responsibility revealed by events. In the first case, he will be more angry precisely because I could and should have been more careful to identify my donkey correctly. The second case seems closer to mere bad luck that could happen to anyone while they were out donkey-shooting, and so the agent seems less responsible. The distinction is not perfect. After all, presumably in the second case as well I could and should have *anticipated* that my donkey might move, and as a result made sure I was close enough to hit him reliably even if and when he did move – and the neighbour might blame me for this particular omission. With the first version, perhaps my neighbour had, unbeknownst to me, recently purchased a donkey that was strikingly similar to mine. I ended up shooting his donkey, but while this is a mistake, it seems close to an "honest" mistake, and the neighbour would be more inclined to withhold blame, given his knowledge of the similarity between the donkeys.

Importantly, I retain *some* moral responsibility regardless of whether it was a mistake or an accident. At the very least, I owe my neighbour an apology. I probably owe him a new donkey. This is no more than the recognition that I caused the damage and therefore I should, as far as possible, bring the resulting situation back to the *status quo ante*. If the damage is irreversible, or the object irreplaceable, then I owe some sort of compensation, although it will depend what I can afford. These are also the underlying principles of tort law, which covers everything from the doctor's mistaken slip of the scalpel to the backpacker's accidental destruction of the porcelain shirehorse in the shop display ("You break it, you've bought it!"). Thus there is an important sense in which a minimal moral responsibility can be derived directly from causal responsibility, regardless of the absence of intention or fault of any kind, and even when such causation is a matter of sheer bad luck. The driving thought is that the damage would not have taken place if you had not been there.

RECKLESSNESS AND NEGLIGENCE

So far we have looked at the *honest* mistake. But many mistakes are *culpable*, even if they are not intentional. The guiding thought is that the mistake arose out of some prior defect of ignorance, inattention or carelessness to a degree short of what the reasonable person would and should know, or attend to, or take care of in the same type of situation. While I am minimally responsible for an honest mistake in the sense that I owe an apology and perhaps compensation, the culpable mistake involves a deeper moral responsibility, one that justifies blame, contempt, resentment, as well as legal penalty. Culpable mistakes can be divided into two kinds with a fuzzy border. Recklessness is when I am aware of the risks but wilfully choose to disregard them. A competent adult kicks a football around with his friends, next to a house. He knows there is a risk of the ball going through a window, but he assumes that his football skills will allow him sufficient control of the ball, but ... He did not intend to break the window, and yet he can be held responsible because he should have made more effort to avoid the risk.

In contrast, negligence is when I am not even aware of the risks. I should be, but for whatever reason I am not, and once again I am blameworthy for this. In the public mind, the word "negligence" is often associated with a medical doctor. The surgeon not only has to know how the plumbing works, but she also has to know all the sorts of thing that can and do go wrong when she sticks the knife in, and what sort of precautions to take to minimize the risks. This requires a certain degree of knowledge, skill and experience. Every procedure in medicine, just as every stage in the doctor's career, is more or less explicitly codified in terms of (slowly evolving) standards of what needs to be known, what needs to be anticipated, what precautions need to be taken. The negligent surgeon is the one who should have known, anticipated, or taken precautions against the risks – but did not, and her negligence directly harms a patient. It is for this harmful failure that she can be held morally responsible.

It is possible to re-conceive recklessness into a species of negligence. Supposedly the reckless footballer "knew" the risks, and chose to disregard them. But it is one thing to know a risk and another to *appreciate* it. The footballer understands the relationship between footballs and glass, but he was more negligent than reckless in genuinely failing to imagine that he would mis-kick the ball. We can understand what appreciation means when we watch the footballer (hopefully) learn from the first reckless incident – the next time he plays footie he can very well appreciate the risks and he goes over to the park. His knowledge of the risks has not changed, but his appreciation has.

Both recklessness and negligence involve norms and standards. The medical norms are those defined by the profession (i.e. based on the nature of the human body and what can be done to it to treat injury, disease and suffering), and regularly tested through the medical student's and doctor's career: in theory, only those who have demonstrated that they understand the relevant norms are allowed to progress to the next stage. The norms about footballs and glass are more general, and can be reasonably expected to be learned as part of the education and upbringing of *every* child, eventually, even the most obtuse.

The minimal responsibility for honest mistakes, and the deeper responsibility for recklessness and negligence, are interesting because they challenge a prevalent assumption among philosophers (and criminal lawyers) that responsibility is centrally a matter of *discrete voluntary acts*. By "discrete", I mean that all the philosophically relevant questions can be answered by looking closely at the act and the agent at the moment of performance. Such a conception relegates omissions and mistakes to a derivative form of responsibility, and one that seems in many respects unfair. The problem, as we saw in the Introduction, is how to link the present to the past when the past no longer exists. The discrete voluntary act conception solves the problem by "pinning" the present blame on the immediate intention as the ultimate source of the evil entering the world. With an unintentional reckless bad act, the blame can be pinned on the past decision to ignore known risks.

But with a negligent bad act, there was – by definition – nothing relevant in the agent's mind at the time of the negligence, so nothing to pin the blame on. As such it was inevitable, *given* his state of mind immediately prior to performing the negligent act, that he would perform it. This seems to come so close to the determinism that characterizes an epileptic fit that it seems grossly unfair to hold the negligent actor responsible. And even if we take the reckless agent as having made a *prior* voluntary decision to ignore the known risks, the fact remains that if we look at the discrete act itself, we can find neither intention nor choice, and this seems to make it unfair to blame him since the act was not sufficiently in his control. It is this sense of unfairness that drives Thomas Nagel's discussion of "moral luck", as we shall see in Chapter 5.

However, once we relax this assumption and start to look at ordinary responsibility attributions in ordinary life, we find that the non-voluntary is just as central and familiar as the voluntary. More importantly, once we relax our assumption that the proper temporal focus is the discrete act, then we start to understand the role of the person – as essentially extended through time – as an equally important locus of reactive attitudes. When judging the reckless footballer, for example, we have one eye on the decision to ignore the risks, another eye on the reckless act itself (the broken window), and a third eye (there are limits to this ocular metaphor) on the footballer's reaction to the broken window.

The footballing example is relatively discrete. So I want to look closer at a favourite topic of the tabloids, the patient's responsibility for his ill health, since this brings in the voluntary and non-voluntary across a much longer span of time, perhaps most of a person's life.

RESPONSIBILITY FOR A RECKLESS LIFESTYLE

In a public healthcare system such as the United Kingdom's, should smokers be held responsible for the health consequences of their reckless choices? The subsidiary question would concern the precise way to hold them responsible: for example, whether they should be asked to contribute financially to the cost of their care, whether their waiting list priority should be reduced, or some other "penalty".

Let us consider the basic principles of the National Health Service. The NHS is funded directly from taxation, and then available to all citizens free of charge at the point of delivery. It is designed to meet the health needs of the nation, and has a principle of treating the patient as they enter the door, without regard for (a) who they are, how wealthy, what race, what sex and so on; (b) how they live, or how they have lived, and (c) how old they are. Basically an individual has a recognizable need and this gives him a right to NHS treatment. (Although there will be questions of his relative priority within the system – if his needs are not life-threatening, then he might not get treatment right away.)

The NHS is not to be thought of as a personal insurance scheme, according to which I put in money while I am healthy in order to be able to draw on it when I am sick. Instead, it is based on solidarity: no matter how much or how little money I have put in, my claims are based on my objective health needs alone. The healthy are forced to contribute to the ill (just as the rich are forced to contribute to the poor via the benefit system) precisely because they are *fellow* citizens. This need not be as altruistic as it sounds: it is after all in the interest of the rich and healthy for the country to have a relatively healthy workforce. But the solidarity is also based on the two-fold egalitarian arbitrariness of illness: (a) almost all of us will get old and will eventually get ill; and (b) most illnesses can strike any of us at any time. In this sense the solidarity is also based on a common vulnerability to ageing and to luck.

So if Prunella is healthy, wealthy and wise, she will be paying a lot of taxes and thereby contributing to the NHS without using it very much. Meanwhile Percy is poor, and spends whatever disposable income he has on booze and fags and junk food and an awful lot of telly. Through his lifetime he will end up contributing little to the NHS's running costs, but will be more and more in need of its services as the booze and fags and junk food and the sedentary lifestyle bring their probable and foreseeable consequences.

Now, although most diseases do not depend on smoking and alcohol, some do, and many diseases will be exacerbated by smoking and drinking. So while it might make sense to treat all appendicitis patients alike, there is a real ethical question about whether to differentiate between the long-term smokers and the non-smokers on the lung cancer ward; whether the obese should be demoted on coronary bypass waiting lists; whether alcoholics should be denied a liver transplant; and whether the threat of delays or denial of treatment should be used to motivate a better – more *responsible* – attitude to one's own health.

In the USA, there is a very different healthcare system. There exist two NHS-style programmes funded by federal taxation: Medicare for the very poor and Medicaid for the elderly. But the programmes are poorly funded and do not reach very many people. Most people have direct private health insurance, or have private insurance mediated through a group scheme organized by their employer (i.e. effectively some of their salary is withheld). Private health insurance differs from NHS provision in two key ways: (a) there are usually several different insurance plans to choose from, so that roughly, the higher premiums one pays, the better treatment one eventually receives; (b) the private insurance company has the right to charge higher premiums depending on one's unhealthy lifestyle.

Left-wing critics of the American system point to the huge numbers of people relying on the underfunded federal programmes, and to the equally huge numbers without any form of insurance at all. Right-wing defenders of the American system will often talk about the value of freedom, including the freedom to make imprudent and short-sighted decisions. But they also speak about the associated value of responsibility in both senses of the word: if the state forces people to take responsibility for their healthcare costs, they will encourage people to take responsibility for their diet and lifestyle, and they will become more responsible – and healthier. The right-wing defender will go on to draw an analogy with home insurance. If I buy a house, there is a risk that it will burn down. So it makes sense to pay for private home insurance: you and other homeowners each put a bit of money in a pot, and when one of your houses burns down, there is money in the pot to cover the cost. Different homeowners will then have the choice of contributing more or less to the pot, depending on how much compensation they want to receive if their house burns down. The state is not involved in the process at all; *nor would anybody expect it to be.* (Or rather, it is involved in the event of extreme natural disasters, and it is involved in procedural monitoring and enforcement of all legal transactions.)[1] So, concludes the right-winger, in the same way that I live in a house and take responsibility for it, I "live" in my body and should be forced to take responsibility for my body and my life.

It is true that introducing a private health insurance system in the UK tomorrow would leave a lot of people bewildered and vulnerable because of their long-standing dependence on the "nanny state". But *over time* people would learn to become more responsible. Every American teenager realizes that part of becoming an adult is learning about health insurance, alongside other financial aspects of life. Every American smoker accepts that they will have to pay not only for the cigarettes but also higher health insurance premiums, which will remind them again and again of the risks they are taking.

The left-winger can respond as follows. First of all, it is possible to make smokers and alcoholics pay extra for their treatment through a carefully calculated luxury or excise tax (it does not seem to be feasible to impose an excise tax on junk food, though). Here it should be noted, however, as with American smokers paying higher premiums, there is still a residual unfairness because the "healthy" smokers will end up subsidizing the "unhealthy" smokers. After all, we are only dealing with probabilities here. A stronger argument against excise taxes is that they are highly regressive: raising the price of a packet of cigarettes from £4 to £5, for example, will have a much greater impact on the financial situation of the poor than on that of the rich.

Second, the left-winger will say that people with unhealthy diets and lifestyles will ultimately be "punished" (both in terms of suffering and, especially, in opportunity costs) by the very diseases to which they are more vulnerable – and that this is punishment enough without taking more money off them or demoting them on the waiting list as well. One's body *is* different from a house in the sense that one needs adequate health if one is to do anything else at all, including owning a house: so the state should be in the business of meeting "fundamental" needs while leaving decisions about meeting more optional needs up to the individual.

The final left-wing argument against holding smokers responsible for the consequences of their reckless lifestyle choices brings us back to the distinction between knowing and appreciating risk. There was a time, maybe fifty years ago, when many people genuinely did not know the link between smoking and later respiratory diseases. But nowadays, nobody can claim that any more. Everybody knows that smoking is bad for you; or at least, that smoking a lot is bad for you. (It is hard to give up smoking when you can argue that *this* one cigarette will have very little impact on your health.) But clearly, it seems, they do not appreciate the dangers they are running, despite the increasingly lurid public information campaigns: either the future is so far away, or else they think naively that they will be one of the lucky few who are not affected by their smoking. Appreciation in this context involves a special kind of imagination, one that might be stirred by a tour of the lung cancer ward, and a chat with a long-term smoker who is now paying the price. (Then again, there are doctors who smoke, doctors who have no problem understanding and appreciating the long-term risks they are running.)

The case of doctors is baffling: are they reckless or do they *intend* to get cancer? This highlights the fuzzy boundary between an intentional act and a reckless act, and I want to explore this boundary with reference to the notorious and tragic English legal case of *Hyam*.[2] Hyam was a woman who had been rejected by her boyfriend, and wanted to take revenge on his new girlfriend. She knew where the girlfriend lived, and went there in the middle of the night with a can of petrol (i.e. she had the presence of mind to prepare the deed, and was not acting in a jealous rage that might ground a later defence of provocation). She poured the petrol through the letter box, and then ignited it with matches and a newspaper, and went away without alerting anyone of the incident. The fire spread, the girlfriend and one of her children managed to get out in time, but two other of her children died in the blaze. In court, Hyam was accused of murder. Hyam accepted that she had been reckless and deserved a manslaughter charge, but argued that her intention had only ever been to scare the girlfriend: she assumed the fire would burn itself out or that the girlfriend would be able to put it out without difficulty. Nevertheless, the House of Lords, on appeal, concluded that there was such a "high possibility" of the fire spreading and killing the house's occupants that any reasonable person lacking murderous intent would have foreseen this possibility and refrained from committing the act. (There are less dangerous ways of getting revenge, after all.) Therefore they were effectively attributing the murderous intent to Hyam and she was sentenced for murder.

There is one detail of English law that needs to be clarified. If a defendant has intended to cause Grievous Bodily Harm (GBH), and the victim dies directly from the injuries inflicted, then the defendant can be charged with murder. The thought is that intending to harm grievously involves such a high probability of death that the intention can be interpreted as "including" death.[3] So in the Hyam case, in rejecting Hyam's claim that she only intended to scare, the Lords were accusing her of having, if not an explicitly murderous intent, then at least an intent to cause GBH. Further evidence for this was her failure to alert the emergency services after the fact, when it might have occurred to someone only intending to scare that they had perhaps gone too far.

The Lords were criticized for this judgment on two grounds, and this criticism was reflected in a change of mind in subsequent judgments. First, it was argued that a "high probability" was not sufficient to indicate intention. In a later judgment[4] responding to a very similar kind of revenge fire-bombing, the Lords insisted on a criterion of "virtual certainty". Second, in evaluating Hyam's actions in comparison to what a reasonable person would have done, they essentially ignored the particular character and beliefs of Hyam herself, that is, they ignored the possibility that it might genuinely not have occurred to her that the house would burn down or that the occupants would not have been able to get out in time. Again, there was no question that she had been reckless and stupid; but without stronger evidence of murderous intention "beyond reasonable doubt" it was unfair to convict her for murder. In later cases[5] the Lords allowed more room for subjective considerations of the agent's precise state of mind.

The debate of the "high probability" of foreseen but unintended consequences links to a larger topic in moral philosophy called the problem of "double effect". The classic example is a bomber pilot fighting a just war. As part of that just war, it has been determined that the most effective thing to bomb is a munitions factory, and that munitions are a legitimate target precisely because they are only designed to aid the enemy's fighting strength. However, the factory is manned and operated by civilian workers, and it is highly probable that some will be killed in the bombing raid. (As non-uniformed non-combatants, the workers are not legitimate targets.) The pilot's primary intention is to destroy the factory – if he could do that without loss of life then he would, and in this sense he does not intend to kill the workers. The principle invites one to think in consequentialist terms: whether the unintended harm was justified by the intended good consequences. The perils of this actuarial approach to ethics should be immediately evident, even if it is not to the people who run modern warfare.[6]

STRICT LIABILITY

We have talked about voluntary acts, and we have talked about honest and culpable mistakes; there is one more category to consider. Strict liability is a legal term, and involves holding the agent legally responsible for a harmful act regardless of his state of mind. It involves the rejection of *all possible* excuses. All that needs to be established is general capacity and causal responsibility. Food producers are strictly liable for the effects of selling contaminated food, even if they had taken all reasonable precautions against the contamination. Licensed owners of dangerous animals are strictly liable for any damage caused by the animal if it gets loose, no matter how secure its cage. Even if a fifteen-year-old girl looks eighteen, behaves like an eighteen-year-old, has credible false identification saying that she is eighteen, and declares her interest in sex with a particular man, then it is still the crime of statutory rape for that man to have sex with her.

Although unfair, strict liability can be justified by a consequentialist argument. In ethics, a consequentialist argument is one that claims to justify one action over another action on the grounds that the first is more likely to generate better consequences than the second. It is the guiding way of thinking in matters of public policy and resource allocation, where the decision-makers want to maximize the benefits created by limited funds. If an extra million pounds appears in the government budget, it is clear that this would be better, morally, to spend on hiring twenty-five nurses for the year than in redecorating the Prime Minister's flat.

A widely known and enforced policy of strict liability means that food producers and tiger-keepers are even more cautious than they might otherwise be tempted to be, and we the public all benefit from that. Now, the response to the consequentialist argument is that it unfairly *uses* an individual to achieve a particular social end; if the tiger gets out and causes damage, then the tiger-keeper is held responsible and punished not for what he did or failed to do (since he was not negligent), but as a way to "set an example": an indirect attempt to modify the behaviour of that keeper and others in the future. And, the critic continues, once we get into the mindset of using individuals to achieve social benefits, there is no restriction in principle on using *any* person in *any* way. (We will encounter consequentialism again in our discussion of punishment in Chapter 4.)

The consequentialist might respond by admitting that strict liability might be unfair on the food producer or tiger-owner, but it is not unfair on the *individual* who freely and knowingly chose to become a food producer or tiger-owner despite the known risks of being held strictly liable for bad luck; and that individual can still withdraw from either occupation any time he wishes. So in that sense the policy is fair, as long as it is publicly known or knowable. (However, this is less plausible with the risk of statutory rape, since it would seem to advocate abstinence except where the partner appears *significantly* over sixteen years of age.)

However, there is an important sense in which the charge of unfairness and the consequentialist response is missing the point. It is not only the fact that we accept the obligation to apologize and sometimes compensate in cases of honest mistakes. It is also a matter about strict liability as a component of role-responsibility. I will have much more to say about this in Part II of this book, but for now, consider the following example from Matravers (2007). A groundsman has been hired to look after the pitch of a football club. The main part of his job is to ensure that the pitch is ready every week for the match on Saturday. Now, there are lots of things that can go wrong – some of them he can anticipate and prepare for, some of them he cannot: maybe he or an important member of his team gets ill, maybe there is torrential rain, maybe there is a fungus attacking the grass, and so on. Technically, all of these could be good excuses for failing to have the pitch ready on time. So it might well be unfair to have a strict liability clause in the employment contract.

But here it is instructive to look at the responsible groundsman's *attitude* to the job, instead of at the framework of the relationship between him, the club's owners and the pitch. The groundsman might have an attitude that expresses the thought: "I'll do my best, I'll work hard, and if something gets in the way, it won't be my fault and the employers will understand." But it is not entirely clear what this statement means because one cannot be precise about "one's best" – one can always do more, after all. And "one's best" might simply not be enough.

A different groundsman might have an attitude that expresses the following thought: "The pitch *must* be ready by Saturday." Already this is interesting because it is not a statement about himself and his "best", but about the pitch, and about what must be done. What he ends up doing is defined by the task, and the standards that dictate when the task has been completed. Whether he has done his "best" is neither here nor there – if the pitch is not ready, then he must do more. Maybe he has to work over-time, maybe he has to cancel other commitments, but he does not see himself as having the choice. More generally, this attitude says something about the spirit within which he works. He is not exchanging his labour for money; rather, he is upholding his commitment simply because it is a commitment. He *then* accepts the money, but the thought of the money is not what motivates him, it is the commitment to the task that "must" get done on time. So here we have a sense of strict liability that is not imposed from the outside, but defines the job from within. It is a risky strategy, however; for if the second groundsman is prevented from completing the task on time, he will take this much more personally than the first groundsman, even if neither are at fault. But there is an important sense in which we admire the second groundsman more than the first (regardless of whether the employers prefer him or not). The notion of such "practical necessity" I will consider again in the section "Huckleberry Finn" in Chapter 7; the notion of unconditional commitments will be relevant to our discussion of parental responsibility in the section "The parent" in Chapter 6. For the moment, however, I want to say something about a piece of English legislation that imposes strict liability on parents.

In England, the Department for Education holds parents responsible for the persistent truancy of their children.[7] This is partly justified on consequentialist grounds: truant children are more likely to get up to mischief without supervision by either parents or schoolteachers. But another justification is paternalistic: the children are being harmed by missing out on their education; that is, the state has a responsibility to take more active measures to keep them in school, on the assumption that they will benefit more from being in school than out. By holding the parents strictly liable, it is assumed that an otherwise indifferent parent will put more effort to exert whatever remaining authority he has over the children's lives. The rub, of course, is that the parents of persistently truant children have probably lost all authority years before, and so are not in a position to do what the reasonable person would do – and for this the legislation has been criticized.

However, I suspect that there is a third justification implicit in the legislation, but never articulated by the politicians who defend it. The parents are to be punished not for what they are failing to do *now*, but for what they failed to do *years ago*, in the early years of their child's life; the parents are implicitly being accused of neglecting their parenting duties and thereby bringing up a child who does not spontaneously understand the point of going to school or appreciate the moral authority of his parents, of schoolteachers, and of the state. The persistent truancy is therefore taken to reveal the parental neglect of long ago. However, this is a very flimsy conclusion to draw from a very complicated process of child-rearing with many causally influential factors beyond parental attention or neglect (on this question, see Le Sage & De Ruyter 2008).

RESPONSIBILITY FOR CHARACTER

This chapter has been about the individual's moral responsibility for culpable mistakes or, in legal terms, for her recklessness and negligence. Some mistakes occur because of stress, distraction or disorientation, and both the agent and the observer can be surprised by the mistake. But a lot of mistakes also result from negative character traits: cowardice, impatience, callousness and especially brute selfishness, and the mistake might fit into a larger pattern within the agent's life. So if we can say that the character trait caused the mistake, and we want to hold the individual responsible for that mistake, we should also be asking whether, and to what degree, the individual is responsible for her character. Indeed, character traits might solve the "pinning" problem of negligence described above, the fact that there does not seem to be anything in the negligent person's head (such as an intention) to "pin" our blame on. Maybe a character trait is what we could blame her for, especially if I can "trace" her present responsibility back to an earlier decision to neglect her character development.

Character comprises a relatively settled collection of relatively settled dispositions to perceive certain things and not others, to deliberate in certain ways, to feel certain emotions in response to certain situations, and finally to act in certain ways. Although the rest of us only perceive the person's actions and utterances, we can infer a good deal about perception, deliberation and emotions, especially if we know the person over a longer period of time. Indeed, part of what it means to know someone is to be able to predict what they would and would not characteristically do in certain situations, as when we exclaim "She would never do that!"

Sometimes our predictions turn out to be incorrect, and sometimes character can change, especially in response to crisis or trauma. But our personal and professional relationships would be unimaginable without a reliable stability of character.

Character is destiny

Questions about character can be framed by two extreme positions. The first is summarized in the dictum "character is destiny": so many of our big choices in life *feel* free at the time we make them, but to others (and to ourselves in retrospect) they seem to fit a pattern. I find myself more "at home" with certain tasks or environments than with others, I find a better "fit" with certain types of people and not others. If I am a loud extrovert, with a thriving social life surrounding team sports, it is unlikely that I will end up working as a historian, with all the solitary archive work that this would demand. It is then tempting to say that I am not *really* free to choose to be a historian, and instead am *destined* to become a football coach, and this lack of control seems to threaten responsibility. Of course I could sign up for a history course for instrumental reasons (to impress my mother), but it is unlikely I would be able to conscientiously cultivate the necessary skills and intellectual stamina to go on to postgraduate study in history.

Behind the dictum that "character is destiny" also lies the assumption that character is unchosen. So much of our character seems to come from our unchosen genetic inheritance and early childhood influences. This seems to double the difficulties in making confident responsibility attributions. Claude examines my cherished porcelain shirehorse in his hands, he drops it, and the shirehorse shatters. How do I respond? My first impulse is to blame him for the lack of care he showed in handling it. But then I remember that he has always been manually clumsy, and I reproach myself for allowing him to handle it in the first place – in so doing I am effectively granting Claude an excuse. But then my second impulse is to blame him for his clumsiness, that is, blame him for a trait that he has possessed over the longer term, and not just for its impact on my shirehorse. I am moving the locus of my blame further back, as it were, and effectively asking him why he did not work harder *in the past* to cultivate greater manual dexterity; at the same time I am hoping that my present rebuke will inspire him to work harder in cultivating dexterity *in the future.* While the result of his clumsiness occupies a relatively narrow slice of time (from two minutes ago until now), as I behold the pieces on the floor, I am taking this as grounds for criticizing a much broader slice of time, deep into the past and future, a much larger segment of Claude's life.

However, my *third* impulse may well be to refrain from blaming Claude altogether. For I am suddenly struck by how pointless it is to blame somebody for something (i.e. failing to cultivate dexterity) from so long ago, and how pointless it is to blame somebody for something that they are unlikely to be able to alter in the future *given* that they have not been able to do it so far. In other words, this third impulse takes the clumsiness to be a permanent trait in Claude, something as permanent as his skin colour, gender and national identity. All I am left with is the high probability that he will be clumsy in the future, and I have to anticipate this and prepare for it as best I can, as if I were preparing for a predicted natural catastrophe.

Scepticism about character

So "character is destiny" is one extreme position that frames any discussion of character. The other extreme is scepticism about whether character is anything but a convenient but ultimately unreliable shorthand for a flimsy entity lacking serious metaphysical or ethical relevance. The brute fact that character traits will not be recognized as a valid excuse in a court of law tells it all. If the defendant tries to say "I couldn't help it, I'm just a coward", this *looks* like a rejection of the Control assumption in the same tone as that which an epileptic would use. And yet the judge can always retort that (a) you shouldn't be a coward, and (b) even if you are, we expect you to *act out of character* when the situation calls for it.[8] The "reasonable person" standard does not demand saintly or heroic action from ordinary people, but it does require a certain minimum which is in principle achievable by all competent adults regardless of their character.

So in discussing responsibility for character we are very much in the context of interpersonal relationships rather than in the courtroom. But even here, the sceptical position takes character concepts to be essentially descriptive without being explanatory: I can describe Claude's *behaviour* at moment 1, at moment 2, at moment 3, and then I can confidently describe the character *disposition* underlying all that behaviour. But in discovering that Claude is clumsy, I am not really adding anything new to my understanding of Claude. I can still ask for an explanation: why is Claude clumsy? It is not clear that this question can be answered, and so all I am left with is the thought that, next time, because Claude is a competent adult, and because all competent adults *should* be careful when handling porcelain shirehorses, that Claude *can* and *will* be careful despite the evidence from similar past occasions, that Claude can be persuaded to be careful (not just to "try" to be careful), that deep down Claude wants to be careful. Thus character scepticism can be closely linked to an essential optimism and hope about the future within the context of non-instrumental relationships.

Aristotle and habituation

Within the limits of the two extremes, Aristotle's notion of "habituation" begins with the thought about tracing responsibility from a present character trait back to an earlier *decision* to fail to attempt to overcome that trait. In Book II of his *Nicomachean Ethics*, Aristotle famously describes how the virtues can be acquired by first *imitating* virtue, and imitating again and again until it sticks. So imagine that I am a minor celebrity (philosophers spend a lot of time imagining these sorts of things) but that I am afraid of heights. Nevertheless I agree to go bungee jumping for a charity event. Up on the bridge, I am a terrified, blubbering wreck: it is even worse than I thought it would be. Nevertheless, I remind myself that my fans are watching, I tell myself that Harry Potter would not be so afraid, I ask myself whether I am a man or a mouse, and so on, I leap … and survive. It was pretty scary, but it turns out it was not as bad as all that. The next time it is a bit easier, and then a bit easier, until I am able to master my fear, and thereby acquire, by choice, the particular physical courage required to bungee jump. Note that courage is not about fearlessness, but about being able to master the right amount of fear, and to master it for a cause whose objective importance is proportional to the known risks involved (i.e. it would not be courageous to run across the M50 motorway just to impress my mates; it would be reckless and stupid). And therefore, says Aristotle, one's character *is* within one's indirect control over the longer term, and cowardice is the necessary result of a previous decision not to work on one's character through habituation. In the same way, one can train one's perceptual faculties in order to notice other people's needs more reliably, one can train one's emotional responses in order to make them more appropriate to the situation, and one can train one's deliberations to go beyond self-interest. And this process not only applies to childhood development, but it continues long into our adult lives as well.

There is clearly some truth to this habituation account, but it cannot be the whole story. For a start, there is the threat of an endless regress: in order to work on a particular character trait, so many other traits already need to be in place: my laziness might prevent me from going to the bungee-jumping to work on my cowardice, for example. Above all, in order to embark on any self-improvement programme, one needs a certain *confidence*. Repeated failures (or what one perceives as failures) can undermine confidence to such an extent that one is convinced there is no point in trying. On the other hand, too much confidence can lead to an arrogant blindness to the traits that still need improvement. And whether or not one has the right degree of confidence can be very much a matter of luck, especially during one's upbringing. So it is too simplistic to say that one is indirectly responsible for all one's character traits, just as it is too simplistic to say that one is responsible for none of them.

Character and the "self-disclosure" account of responsibility

Retrospective responsibility is typically about individuals committing *acts*. Prospective responsibility is typically about individuals performing *roles* and carrying out *duties* defined by those roles. Both these kinds of responsibility are obvious and familiar, and the criminal and tort law can be understood as an attempt to flesh out our ordinary intuitions governing responsibility attributions of either kind in ordinary situations. However, there is a third kind of responsibility which does not fit easily into the legal paradigm, and perhaps for that reason has received less attention from philosophers. It is the phenomenon that Gary Watson (1996) calls responsibility as self-disclosure, which dates back to a conception first elaborated by David Hume.[9]

The challenge comes from certain situations where we are inclined to say that the agent should not be held fully responsible because she was not behaving *in character*. Afterwards the individual will typically apologize, adding something like "I don't know what got into me" or "I'm really not like that at all". Perhaps the individual was stressed or distracted or grieving. Perhaps the individual was drunk, although we have to be careful because drunkenness can either distort character into puerile exhibitionism or it can reveal character (*"in vino veritas"*). Hypnosis is a striking example of acting out of character, precisely because one's will is overridden by that of an identifiable foreign agent.

Now, when stressed or distracted or grieving, we are still competent and in control for the purposes of retrospective act-responsibility and prospective role-responsibility. The distraction and grief is not enough to remove competence and thereby exculpate in a court of law (although it may mitigate). Importantly, the individual herself can admit act-responsibility (and accept the obligation to offer apologies and reparations) while at the same time denying that she was "deeply" responsible. The act was hers in that she did it, but it was not hers in that it did not express her identity, her character or her deepest values. In that sense, we might say, she can "accept" responsibility without "taking" responsibility. Correspondingly, one might find oneself willing to apologize in a shallow way for what one did, but be sufficiently baffled about how one did it to prevent one from apologizing in a deeper sense. This is a phenomenon I consider in the next chapter.

3

APOLOGY AND FORGIVENESS

Let us return to the paradigmatic "blame game" encounter around which this whole book is structured. We have one individual who does something wrong; we have another individual (the victim) who is inclined to blame or resent or be angry at her *for* the wrong. Such blame made three assumptions about the wrongdoer's capacity, control and understanding of what she was doing. The next move is then the wrongdoer's. She may deny causal responsibility altogether, and provide further details to reveal why the accusation was incorrect. If she accepts causal responsibility but not moral responsibility, she will already owe a minimal apology to express her regret that the wrong was caused, but then go on to offer an excuse or justification for the wrong. Alternatively, she may accept causal and moral responsibility, in which case she owes the victim a deeper apology. Then the game moves back to the victim, and she has to decide how to respond to the excuse, to the deep apology, or to the defiant lack of apology – and one option open to her will be to forgive the wrongdoer for wronging her. This chapter will therefore investigate the wrongdoer's apology and the victim's forgiveness.

In the last thirty years of Anglo-American philosophy, there has been much more interest in forgiveness than in apology. Perhaps philosophers assume that apology is not an important step in the game: either the offender apologizes or he doesn't, and either way the most interesting question is how the victim should respond. I think that apologies can be a little more philosophically problematic, and can reveal something interesting about the complex nature of the enduring self's relationship with the past.

APOLOGY

Nick Smith (2008) has written the most detailed philosophical study on the nature of apologies, and I shall be drawing on this in what follows. The words "I'm sorry" can of course be used in a non-apologetic sense for things I had no causal relationship to, and these are perhaps better described as expressions of sympathy and condolence: "I'm sorry to hear about your mother". Next, we have those situations where "I'm sorry" is used in situations where I *did* cause harm, but without recklessness or negligence: "Sorry I'm late, the plane was delayed". This minimal apology corresponds to the "minimal responsibility" I described in the section "Recklessness and negligence" in Chapter 2, such that the apology signifies an acknowledgement of strict liability: whatever my excuse, the apology was owed, and perhaps compensation as well. Beyond these two types, the concept of apology becomes more philosophically interesting. When I am at fault – and *accept* that I am at fault – then I owe what Smith calls a "categorical" apology, and this involves fourteen conditions, the most important of which for my purposes are the following:

- *An explanation condition.* The apology will be accompanied by an account and an explanation of what happened and why, where such an account will include details of the offender's mental states, such as beliefs, desires and intentions (Smith 2008: 28).
- *A blame condition.* The offender must accept that the act was wrong, she must acknowledge causal and moral responsibility for the harm done to the victim, and she must accept blame for the act (*ibid.*: 34, 42).
- *A redress condition.* The offender "takes practical responsibility for the harm she causes, providing commensurate remedies

and other incommensurable forms of redress to the best of her abilities" (*ibid.*: 142).

- *A non-recidivism commitment.* The offender experiences and expresses "categorical regret". This involves: (a) the sincere wish that she had not done the act (the remorse criterion); (b) "In accordance with this realisation she commits to not making the same mistake again" (*ibid.*: 68).

Importantly, says Smith, any apology meeting the above conditions might not be a complete step in the blame game; instead, it might be the beginning of a conversation about the content of the apology, since the victim might not be satisfied by the quality of the explanation, but by the sincerity of the acceptance of blame, by the quantity or quality of redress, or by the strength of the non-recidivism commitment. In other words, the victim might not be clear enough in her mind about the precise relationship between the wrongdoer and the wrong during this apologetic step in the blame game, and so she might not yet be ready to embark on the next step of whether to forgive or not. The nature of this conversation might depend on standards of reasonableness, which could be perhaps invoked by calling upon a third party to rule on a persistent disagreement. On the other hand, the nature of the conversation might also depend on unique aspects of the antecedent relationship between wrongdoer and victim, and in that case a mutually satisfactory resolution to the blame game might depend on a host of contingent factors that could be unintelligible to third parties.

So, for example, part of my apology for forgetting your birthday might be to explain my previous mental state thus: "I didn't realize it was so important to you". And this might well add insult to injury! Instead of being harmed by the forgetting, you are harmed even more by the non-awareness of the birthday's importance. Should I then apologize for this non-awareness? Maybe the non-awareness was caused, you believe, by an even more general pattern of not taking you seriously enough. And maybe this was caused by my lack of sufficient emotional maturity to handle an adult relationship. At each stage the "offence" seems to swell, and it is less and less clear how I am to apologize for something so big, and indeed whether I can apologize for it at all. An alternative way to put it would be: the more explanation I seek and provide, the less we are talking about what I have *done* and the more we are talking about what I *am*. And it is not at all clear whether I can apologize for what I am, since there is not enough distance between the apologizer and the thing that I am apologizing for. (I will say more about the metaphor of distance, below.)

In a similar vein, the conversation that takes place after the first apology might reveal certain of my central commitments and values. So imagine that I missed your birthday party because of a last-minute request from my boss after hours. I was under no obligation to help my boss, but the job and my career are important to me. I know that I promised to be at your birthday party, and I certainly did not want to miss it, but in this situation it was clear that I had to miss it. Again, you are upset, and are not impressed with my apology. You would prefer it if my job and career were less important to me. In this conversation, however, I learn nothing new about you: I knew full well that you would be upset, just as I knew that my reason for missing your birthday party would not impress you. And yet I chose to miss the birthday party, and moreover, if I were in the same situation again, I would choose to miss the birthday party again – as such I cannot fulfil the non-recidivism condition for a categorical apology. The job and the career are so important to me, and to my sense of self, that I cannot apologize for them. All I can do is express a minimal apology, which expresses no more than my regret that I was placed in the situation where I ended up breaking my promise to you. (I also have to prepare myself, of course, for the possibility that my refusal to compromise on this matter might be taken as a last straw in your own deliberations about whether to stay in a relationship with me at all.)

In making categorical regret central to his account, Smith accepts that he differs from other commentators, such as Lazare (2005). The latter is interested primarily in the question of redress, that is, what we might call the "cash value" of the apology. The apology (and with it the feeling of responsibility) is sufficiently sincere if the offender is willing to compensate the victim, to pay for the damages, or to make it up to the victim in some other way. A redress-focused apology still acknowledges wrongdoing and accepts blame, but there is no essential need to take *retrospective* responsibility, in the sense that there is no need for an explanation by the offender or understanding by the victim about how or why the harm was caused, beyond whatever minimal description might be necessary to calculate the required redress. As such this redress-focused apology is essentially forward-looking. Indeed, as Smith says, there is not even any need for categorical regret. Redress-focused apologies are obviously very important for law, politics and society, or in cases where, for whatever reason, I cannot remember the details of the act or of my mindset at the time.

The categorical apology looks both forward and backward. Redress and non-recidivism is still important, but equally important is regret and explanation, or at least a willingness to have a conversation prompted by my explanation. Usually the interpersonal situation will begin with the victim's perplexity ("Why on earth did you do that to me?").

Smith's account of categorical apology can accommodate the following cases: (a) I make an honest (that is, non-negligent) mistake: I was ignorant at the time that my action was harming you, and only now do I understand the full picture; I'm sorry; (b) if I did knowingly harm you it was because I honestly thought I was justified in doing so, but now I see – because of new evidence or new arguments – that I was not; I'm sorry. In both cases I care about you, and about your good opinion of me, so I do not just ignore the harm, I seek you out to explain and apologize. However, strictly speaking, in these cases I am not apologizing for the act or for my ignorance since there was no negligence in either; I am only apologizing for the harm for which I accept I was directly responsible. I do not regret *choosing* one way or another, I regret what happened as a result of my ignorant choice. Bernard Williams in his article "Moral Luck" (1981d: 28) famously described this kind of regret as *agent-regret*, and distinguished it from remorse, where I regret having knowingly wronged someone, and from spectatorial regret, where I was not causally involved but where I wish that the harm had not happened. (I will be discussing agent-regret and moral luck in Chapter 5, § "Williams's lorry-driver and Gauguin".)

Smith can also accommodate apologies for the consequences of earlier decisions made on the basis of sincere values with which I no longer identify. In Tolstoy's 1886 short story *The Death of*

Ivan Illych, Ivan Illych is a successful career man who neglects his family. Then he falls ill, re-evaluates his life, and comes to consider his family much more important. He apologizes to his wife and children for neglecting them. It is not only that he distances himself from the neglectful actions, he also distances himself from the values and priorities – and the *person* – who caused them.

So far I am in full agreement with Smith. But in the following I want to present two specific counter-examples which I feel his account cannot accommodate. In both cases the person does something wrong, knows she has done something wrong, but feels that she cannot honestly apologize for it – and not out of fear or arrogance or other motives unrelated to the action and any harm caused. In each example the wrongdoing is deliberate and informed (not a mistake), and does not involve a hard choice between two incompatible actions, both of which would involve wrongdoing. In one case I want to argue that despite the wrongdoer's best efforts, the past act can remain *too obscure*, where the obscurity is not due to amnesia or to temporal distance or to self-deception. In the second case, the problem is the opposite: the wrongdoing is *too familiar*, and the wrongdoer knows exactly why he did it.

Example 1: the act is too obscure

Apologizing for something requires two moments in time: at t_1 the person performs the act and at t_2 she judges it to have been harmful and takes responsibility by apologizing for it. Without begging questions about personal identity, I want to speak of two selves: the judging self at t_2 and the judged self at t_1. Between t_1 and t_2 there is full spatiotemporal bodily continuity and full psychological continuity, and the self at t_2 can remember experiencing the world at t_1. Even though I can vividly remember performing the act, it can still be difficult to understand. I have in mind such common experiences as when we say "What the hell was I thinking of?" or "What got into me?" In such cases, I, the remembering self, am unable to enter the mindset of my past self sufficiently to understand why I did it. While I can take minimal responsibility for the harmful consequences of the act, this can never be accompanied by anything more than a redress-focused, forward-looking apology. And because the act is not intelligible enough on its own, I cannot claim sufficient authority to apologize, as it were, on behalf of the past agent. And because I am mystified by the volitional origins of the act, I cannot sincerely commit myself to its not happening again. All I can do is hope that it will not happen again, and try to influence my actions indirectly, for example, by avoiding the situations in which the act took place. It is as if the action belongs to someone else – someone I am responsible for, certainly, but more in the way that I might be strictly liable for the destructive actions of my unruly young child or dog.

Agnes has been married to Bertram for seven years, they have no children, and things are going well enough. On a business trip, Agnes meets an attractive man and spends the evening flirting with him over dinner. After dinner, she thinks for a moment, and then decides to initiate the business that will culminate in his hotel bedroom overnight. Afterwards she feels badly about it, and when she returns home she confesses everything to Bertram. However, she finds that she is unable to categorically apologize. It is important to see that Agnes's inability is not a refusal. When someone refuses to apologize, it may be because they deny culpability, or they see their act as justified, or they see the victim as having deserved the harm or as over-reacting to a harmless act. In contrast, Agnes accepts that the act was a wrong against Bertram, she knew it would be harmful to Bertram, and she accepts his right to be angry and indignant. She could have reached for an excuse by claiming that she was overwhelmed by passion or drink, but she wasn't. She could have reached for a justification by arguing in favour of an open marriage, but she doesn't believe in that.

A different Agnes might have been genuinely surprised by Bertram's response, and felt ashamed: the shame would then constitute a revelation of the moral reality of what she had done, and she could be said to have learned something from what turned out to be a terrible mistake that she honestly did not appreciate at the time (and she may have been all the more fortified in her sincere intention never to do it again). Such an Agnes could categorically apologize. But our Agnes was not surprised by Bertram's reaction, and learned nothing new from the conversation. Another different

Agnes might have deceived herself into the infidelity, by saying that "Bertram would understand" or "Bertram will forgive". But our Agnes was completely honest with herself about what she was doing, and about the hurt it would cause Bertram; and she does not consider herself entitled to forgiveness. If Bertram is upset and leaves her, she would not be surprised and would not blame him.

And here is the problem of distance. While she can apologize in a forward-looking redress-oriented way, she cannot apologize categorically to Bertram because she cannot identify enough with her past self. In one sense, of course, she knows full well "what got into her" and "what the hell she was thinking": there is nothing obscure about sexual lust and adventure. But normally her desire for sexual pleasure would not be a good enough reason to indulge it; indeed, normally she would not even have allowed the thought to form into a temptation. She does not understand and she cannot explain how it got the better of her that night; even if it was not an "it" that got the better of her, she remembers choosing, freely and knowingly. In addition, she feels it would be *impudent* to apologize to Bertram, for she would not be able to back the apology up with a sincere repentant commitment to refrain from such stray acts in the future: if it happened once, she "has it in her" to do it again, and she realizes that Bertram would be entitled to the same thought.

This example suffers from one strong weakness: it concerns a marriage, and marriages are probably the most impenetrable objects in the universe, even to their direct participants. There might be an explanation for Agnes's infidelity if, say, a marriage counsellor had hours and hours to spend rummaging through the three accounts of husband, wife, and husband and wife together. For my purposes, all I really need is the exasperated exclamation "What got into me?" As long as Agnes cannot understand the action of her past self, then I suggest she is deprived of the possibility of categorically apologizing.

Example 2: the act is too familiar[1]

I now want to consider the opposite problem. Once again, let us consider our two-self schema: the present person at t_2 judges the past self, who performed a harmful action at t_1. This time, however, he finds that the past self is too familiar, that there is not enough distance between the present and the past, that the present self has not moved on sufficiently to take up an authoritative critical stance required for categorical apology. In invoking this metaphor of distance, I am drawing on the earlier mention of the difficulty of apologizing for who one is. In the normal model of criticism, two separate people interact in one timeframe: I criticize you for performing the harmful act. In order for me to avoid hypocrisy, that is, in order to achieve the authoritative critical stance, I have to at least sincerely believe – at the moment of uttering the criticism – that I would not have performed the act in the same circumstances in which you performed it. This involves a distance between us; not so much a spatial distance but a moral distance. So if we turn to the two-self model, then the later self requires a certain moral distance to criticize the earlier self without hypocrisy; he needs to have moved on. If he does not move on, then he still has it in him to perform the harmful act again, and this undermines any attempt at a categorical apology.

Two friends, Crispin and Darina, are walking home late one night when they are confronted by a skinhead, evidently drunk and looking for a fight. Crispin knows he is a good runner, and runs. Darina is overweight and less athletic, and is easily apprehended by the skinhead, who beats her up and robs her. After phoning the police, Crispin watches from the distance, horrified. As the skinhead slouches off into the night, Crispin rushes back to Darina to see if she is all right. Darina is furious, and shouts, "Get your hands off me, you bloody coward. If you'd stayed, the two of us could have shaken him off, but on my own I didn't stand a chance." Crispin is deeply ashamed. He thinks about the episode all week. He desperately wants to apologize to Darina, but Darina does not answer her phone. However, the more Crispin thinks about it, the more he finds that he would not be able to apologize even if Darina were receptive.

The thing is, although this was an entirely new situation for Crispin, he finds that it fits with a settled pattern of physically cowardly behaviour in much of his life. He knows what he should have done, on this and other occasions; he certainly does not deny his cowardice. And yet he also knows that if he were to find himself in the same situation in the future, he would behave in exactly the same way, but not because he would *choose* to do so. He knows his fear is exaggerated, or that his fear is appropriate but he cannot overcome it – in that sense he does not endorse his response. So when his present self looks back on the past cowardly self, he finds that there is no moral distance; he has remained the same, and he is able to fully identify with his past self and to recognize full ownership of the action.

Because he has not moved on sufficiently from his former self, he does not have the authority required to criticize it fully. To invoke Augustine's famous distinction, he cannot hate the sin and love the sinner, because the sin came out of the sinner, revealed the sinner for what he was – and still is. If confronted by the skinhead again, he would run again, that is just the way he believes he is made. To put it another way, Crispin feels bad about what he did, but he cannot call this bad feeling remorse, for he cannot intelligibly wish that he had not done it. If he feels remorse now, why did he not feel, as it were, anticipatory remorse then, a remorse that would have silenced any reasons or inclinations to run? Even though Crispin genuinely believes that he is "made that way", he also knows that he cannot apologize on the basis of an excuse, precisely because, as we saw in the last chapter, a vice does not let one off the hook in the way a handicap can.

FORGIVENESS

We have seen some of the complexities involved in apologies. Let us now consider the apology to have been made, and we pass onto the next step in the blame game, where the victim has to respond. One available response is to forgive the wrongdoer for the wrong, in so far as the victim is able to do so; but such forgiveness might require the fulfilment of certain conditions. If the forgiveness is granted, what does this do to the wrong and to the relationship between the wrongdoer and the victim – does it "wipe the slate clean"? In this section I want to examine what forgiveness is exactly, and what sort of conditions, if any, might be relevant to its granting, and what the forgiveness achieves. Ultimately, I want to show that forgiveness involves a kind of "taking responsibility" for the harm – and for the wrongdoer, where such a "taking" may depend on the particular victim's unique perspective on the wrongdoer and the harm.

Before we can start to answer these questions, we have to distinguish forgiveness from certain other responses to wrongdoing, namely excusing, ignoring and forgetting. Each of these terms is to be taken in its interpersonal context, rather than in the legal context, precisely because the law does not recognize the victim's option to forgive. When a crime has been committed, it is committed against society, and it is society who must respond through the criminal justice system, regardless of whether or not the victim forgives the wrongdoer. Indeed, it is perfectly compatible for a victim to forgive, but at the same time to be satisfied that the wrongdoer is punished because the victim believes that the crime simply *should* be punished, or that the wrongdoer will somehow benefit from the punishment. So, here are some points that will help us to distinguish the terms:

- If a *prima facie* wrong turns out to be justified in the big picture, then there is no wrong and therefore nothing to forgive.
- If the wrongdoer can offer a valid excuse (i.e. the noun) that reduces his moral responsibility for the wrong, then the appropriate response is not to forgive but to *excuse* (i.e. the verb). Many minor mistakes and accidents involve superficial apologies and superficial forgiveness ("that's all right"), which are nonetheless important in lubricating social interaction of all kinds.
- Sometimes the wrongdoer commits an inexcusable wrong, but it is relatively minor and the appropriate response is simply to *ignore* it – I am thinking of all the petty acts of greed, selfishness, spite or cruelty that one encounters during an ordinary day; or sometimes I have to get along with a work colleague or a family member even if he does not like me and wants to trip me up.
- We should be careful of the expression "forgive and forget". The link between forgiving and forgetting might draw some

of its plausibility from the metaphor of forgiving a *debt*: the debt is cancelled and can indeed be forgotten. Now, one can ignore a minor wrong long enough to eventually forget it, especially when one has other things to worry about, or when one is used to a rough-and-tumble atmosphere of continuous political tension. But in such cases one has not forgiven, and the wrongdoing has not been eliminated. In contrast, when I forgive something, I do not forget it, and arguably should not forget it; instead I hold the wrongdoer responsible while attempting to change my attitude towards him.

- By forgiving, the victim can loosen the resentful hold that the offence has on him. Sometimes there can be good therapeutic reasons to forgive, if the alternative is incapacitating bitterness. The self-help literature is full of recommendations to forgive, but it is important to see that such recommendations often amount to little more than ignoring or looking on the bright side. Genuine forgiveness has to involve some sort of active engagement with the wrongdoer and the wrong.

So what is forgiveness, then? The decision to forgive involves the conscious attempt to prevent one's spontaneous and morally legitimate resentment from influencing one's thoughts about the wrongdoer, where such an attempt must be based on some *new understanding* of him and of the offence. The decision to forgive must also be manifest in certain characteristic types of friendly action or gesture, and by the refusal to seek revenge. Let me stress two things in this definition. First, from the victim's point of view, we can only speak of an attempt; it may turn out that the attempt has to be repeated or sustained over a longer period, or indeed that it fails despite the victim's best efforts. Perhaps the victim thinks he has forgiven, and then three months later the resentment suddenly returns in full force after a reminder of the wrong; in such a case the wrongdoer could legitimately say: "I thought you'd forgiven me!" Second, the resentment is morally legitimate in the sense that such a response is compatible with justice; I am assuming, for the moment, that the victim has been genuinely wronged. In contrast, I am not talking about my spontaneous resentment of a police officer for justly fining me for speeding!

Before I continue in this chapter, one important reminder of the scope of this book: I will mainly be considering ordinary and familiar offences here, committed in the politically stable and wealthy modern West, and in familiar contexts such as school, work, democratic politics, marriage, and so on. Much of the philosophical literature on forgiveness concerns egregious wrongs such as those perpetrated within the context of the Holocaust or South African Apartheid, and I find it difficult to rely on my moral intuitions with any confidence in such discussions, partly since I have no direct experience of the events in question. Would or should I myself forgive my torturer? I have absolutely no idea.

Griswold's account

Charles Griswold's book (2007) offers one of the most recent and certainly one of the most systematic and subtle analyses of forgiveness. He follows a number of philosophers[2] who claim that forgiveness must be *norm-governed* and *conditional*. Conditionality means that the wrongdoer must fulfil some conditions in order to "earn" the forgiveness; if the victim nevertheless goes ahead and forgives the wrongdoer without the latter's fulfilment of these conditions, then the victim is doing something wrong (*ibid.*: 63–4). The main condition can be summarized by the word "repentance". What does repentance mean? Griswold outlines six conditions in a "paradigmatic case", and they resemble Smith's definition of a categorical apology. Here are the first two:

- "the wrong-doer's demonstration that she no longer wishes to stand by herself as the author of those wrongs";
- "she must repudiate her deeds (by acknowledging their wrongness) and thus disavow the idea that she would author those deeds again" (*ibid.*: 49–51).

Griswold considers the possibility of "hating the sin and loving the sinner", as if the wrongdoer approaches the victim and invites him to jointly condemn the aberration. But Griswold is right to reject this: first, because it sounds like the wrongdoer is asking to be excused rather than forgiven; second, because the wrongdoer should be asking to be forgiven precisely *for the offence* – in being morally responsible for the offence, he is conceptually linked to the offence. Loosening the ties of moral responsibility for one's freely chosen past actions threatens to undermine too many important components of people's lives, such as promises and debts, not to mention contracts and friendships. Griswold continues:

- she "must experience and express regret at having caused that particular injury to that particular person";
- she "must commit to becoming the sort of person who does not inflict injury, and that commitment must be shown through deeds as well as words";
- she "must show that she understands, from the injured person's perspective, the damage done by the injury";
- "the wrongdoer's regretful address would offer some sort of narrative accounting for how she came to do wrong" (*ibid.*: 49–51).

The other thing that forgiveness has to be, according to Griswold, is norm-governed. Norm-governance means that the repentant wrongdoer "earns" or "qualifies for" the forgiveness, that forgiveness has become "appropriate", and that the victim is "entitled" to forgive, in accordance with relevant norms (these scare quotes refer to Griswold's terms). For a clue about the nature of these norms, Griswold looks to the etymology of the word "forgive", and argues that the practice of *giving* is norm-governed in a similar way (*ibid.*: 63). When I am invited to dinner, there are norms governing the sort of gift to bring, the amount of money to spend on the gift, the presentation of the gift, and so on. Such norms do not require a specific gift on a specific occasion: they delimit a space of appropriateness within which I am free to give whatever I want. I should bring a bottle, not a hamster, for example. The bottle should not be embarrassingly expensive or cheap. Now, importantly, I can also refuse to give the gift, although I may be blameworthy for doing so: I may be rightly described as a cheapskate or a sponger, and I may not be invited to any further dinners (*ibid.*: 67). As such, concludes Griswold, a gift differs from a debt. With a gift there is some room for choice, including the choice to disregard the gift-giving norms entirely, albeit at some cost. In contrast, a debt has a more specific content, and if I refuse to pay my debt I am still indebted whether I like it or not.

As with giving, so with forgiving, says Griswold. The conditions still allow some room for me to choose how exactly to forgive, and they also allow room for me to refuse to forgive even after the wrongdoer has done all he can to repent. When I refuse to forgive the genuinely repentant wrongdoer, I am then liable to be blamed by a third party for being "unforgiving", unreasonably demanding, or even hard-hearted. In this way Griswold hopes to accommodate two *prima facie* incompatible intuitions: (a) that forgiveness should be elective rather than owed; (b) that it makes sense for a third party to tell the victim that he "ought to" forgive the wrongdoer, or indeed for the victim to ask himself whether he ought to forgive.

In arguing for conditional forgiveness, Griswold is directly opposing accounts of unconditional forgiveness, the most famous example of which is, of course, a popular conception of Christianity. The Christian victim is supposed to forgive regardless of whether the wrongdoer apologizes or repents, indeed regardless of whether the wrongdoer sees himself as having done anything wrong at all. The Christian is supposed to remember that he himself is just as much of a fallible sinner as the wrongdoer, and that the wrongdoer is just as much of a child of God as he is himself. ("Forgive our trespasses as we forgive those [– unconditionally –] who have trespassed against us.") Griswold describes two serious problems with unconditional forgiveness. First, it risks condoning evil, as if to say: "It's all right, it doesn't really matter, I don't care whether you do it again." For Griswold, if the wrongdoer fails to repent, these are grounds for the vigorous condemnation which evil deserves. Second, it risks self-denigration, as in the battered wife who effectively expresses, again and again, the thought: "It's all right, I forgive you, I don't really deserve anything better than this." The refusal to forgive the unrepentant wrongdoer is the first step in repossessing one's self-respect and demanding to be treated seriously: in the case of a battered wife, it is the first step to leaving the marriage.

Criticism of Griswold's account

Griswold's etymological analysis is useful, and I would also like to help myself to it in order to launch my criticism of his account. Let us return to the dinner party, bottle in hand. I want to argue that the bottle is *not* a gift in the full sense of the word. Why not? Not because there are no norms, but because the norms are too present in the consciousness of the donor and the beneficiary. The donor thinks: "It's quite a formal do, I'd better bring a bottle", or perhaps: "That was awkward, I should have brought something a little more expensive". The host expects the bottle or something equivalent, notices its absence; perhaps he smiles, but he makes a mental note. I want to suggest that this is not the appropriate psychology of genuine gift-giving, nor is it the psychology of the supererogatory, for example of altruism, heroism and virtue. The genuinely courageous person is not conscious of his courage at the moment he performs the courageous action – all he is thinking about is what must be done. At the same time, courage is of course subject to external norms. D. Z. Phillips puts it well in his discussion of the psychology of caring:

> Is not the form of the imperative "You ought to heed these considerations if you care or if you are interested"? This is not so. To think otherwise is to confuse the conditions under which a man has reasons for paying attention to moral considerations with his paying attention. He will not have such reasons unless he cares, but the fact that he cares is not his reason for caring. If, hurrying to the cinema, I stop to help the victim of an epileptic fit, while it is true that, in the absence of considerations of personal advantage, I should not have stopped unless I cared, it does not follow that my reason for helping him is because I care. The reason is to be found in the suffering of the epileptic. (Phillips 1992: 133)

In contrast to the dinner guest, the donor of a genuine gift has no expectations; the gift is in no way a payment, an investment, a lubricant; it has nothing prudential or self-regarding at all. It is true that an experienced person will be better able to read a situation, and to discern the beneficiary's needs and wants, and his gift will therefore be more appropriate. But whether it is a gift in the first place will be a question of the donor's psychology.

Similarly, when a person receives a genuine gift, he does not allow (as far as possible) thoughts of expectation, appropriateness and cheapskatedness to enter his mind, and he does not look the proverbial gift-horse in the mouth. Of course such thoughts may enter his mind, but he does not endorse them, in the same way that a person refuses to endorse other embarrassing thoughts (racist, cruel, sexually perverse) that stray into his mind. Rather, he is moved by the generous intention behind the gift. All this is compatible with Griswold's norms: the gift may well be inappropriate for any number of reasons.

It might be objected that the donor expects, if nothing else, at least gratitude. This is true, but such gratitude is not an object which is returned to the donor as part of the transaction, just as it is not an object that fills the donor's mind as the end he pursues in giving the gift. (And despite what implausible reductionist accounts would have us believe, the genuine donor is not in search of the "charity buzz".) The genuine donor is motivated only by the apparent needs and desires of the beneficiary; and the beneficiary's gratitude is no more than the recognition of the gift as a gift: the donor expects gratitude only as confirmation that the gift got through. At the extreme will be the gifts offered by saints, where not even gratitude will be expected; for saints, giving is entirely selfless, and yet paradoxically the gifts in question express the donor's self in an especially pure fashion. Of course most of us cannot achieve such selflessness, and so my account is one of degrees rather than absolutes. At one end is the pure economic transaction, at the other the saint's selfless donation: in between runs a continuum upon which the given object has greater or lesser gift-like status.

My argument against Griswold is that by focusing on gift-giving norms and disregarding psychology, he seems to allow all actions on this continuum the status of gift: for even in crude economic exchanges he would probably perceive sufficient electivity (in both having a range of appropriate options, and having the freedom to defy the norms). But such basic electivity is not enough to confer gift-like status.

Now, in the same way that "gift" is used in a thin sense to denote my entrance ticket to the dinner party, so too can "forgiveness" be used in a thin sense as social lubrication. There is nothing wrong with such courteous exchanges, and our social world would be impossible without allowing face-saving ways of dissipating momentary friction. The most primitive exchange rituals are those of "please" and "thank you" taught to pre-school children, which then move on to reconciliatory expressions such as "I'm sorry" and "It's all right". There might be a moment's suspicion of malice, but most people can give the benefit of the doubt and move on, without anything so clumsy or formal as robust forgiveness. Such practices, as we saw in Chapter 1, are better described as the offering and receiving of excuses.

Because of its supererogatory status, genuine forgiveness cannot be expected or assumed, and especially not by the wrongdoer, regardless of how many of Griswold's conditions he manages to tick off. Instead, the wrongdoer has to be genuinely unsure about whether he will be forgiven or not, and indeed genuinely unsure of whether the victim wants to have anything further to do with him. After all, what is the point of forgiveness, what does it achieve, if it is to function as no more than a rhetorical full stop to a process that is initiated and concluded by the wrongdoer along reliable lines? This question is similar to that voiced in discussions about a theory of punishment, as we shall see in the next chapter: if the wrongdoer is genuinely repentant, what is the point of punishing him? Griswold believes that the modicum of electivity he vouchsafes the victim can provide the space for achievement, but I suggest this is small beer.

Indeed, Griswold's emphasis on conditions comes too close to *indecency* in two opposite ways: on the one hand, the impatient wrongdoer who says: "Come on, come on, I've fulfilled all the conditions, now give me what I have earned"; on the other, the imperious victim waiting for the conditions to be fulfilled before handing down his forgiveness. As Garrard and McNaughten put it:

> In our view, to forgive involves not requiring apology
> or penance. To insist on an apology is to insist that the

wrongdoer humble himself before one, and this implies that there is still some residual resentment. Any relishing of the wrongdoer's lowered standing in relation to the forgiver impugns the genuineness of the forgiveness. And similar remarks apply to insisting on penance.

(Garrard & McNaughton 2003: 47)

In response to these two scenarios of indecency, however, Griswold could offer an equally disturbing scenario implied by the unconditional account. The wrongdoer offends, and then attempts to do everything to be forgiven, not in the arrogant way described above but in humble good faith; he is genuinely repentant, feels terribly guilty, and is desperate to re-establish the relationship with the victim. And yet the victim will not forgive. Indeed, the wrongdoer could be refused forgiveness for even trivial and unintended slights. Surely there is an enormous risk here of sheer bloody-minded stubbornness on the part of the victim, or for preciousness and vanity? Surely it is implausible to place so much power in the hands of the victim, without any accompanying pressure on the victim to account for the decisions resulting from his power? Surely the victim is not infallible or immune to criticism on this matter?

Garrard and McNaughton's unconditional account

In the previous section I gave some reasons for challenging Griswold's account and for favouring the "Christian", unconditional account. In this section I want to consider – but ultimately reject – one account of unconditional forgiveness, that of Garrard and McNaughton (2003) (henceforward G&M). G&M argue that genuine forgiveness should not depend on the wrongdoer fulfilling general or specific conditions. However, they argue for a different set of conditions, this time on the victim rather than on the wrongdoer. For genuine forgiveness, the victim has to be motivated only by a sense of "human solidarity", by an awareness of the common vulnerability that he shares with the wrongdoer (*ibid.*: 54).[3] Such an awareness partly comprises a generous imaginative acknowledgement that I, too, might have committed the same type of offence in the same type of circumstances. And even when I cannot imagine myself committing that type of offence in that type of circumstances, solidarity involves imagining myself having become the person that might have committed it – *if* my early and ongoing circumstances had been less favourable. And since we can never be sure about such hypothetical life histories, conclude G&M, we should give the benefit of the doubt, and forgive unconditionally.

G&M's account therefore rejects Griswold's conditionality but accepts the need for normative guidance of some sort, that is, it accepts Griswold's intuition that the victim can be legitimately subject to moral criticism for failing to forgive, although here that means failing to have or to exercise sufficient imagination and humility to appreciate the brute contingency of the interaction between himself and the wrongdoer. This account also generates reasons which the victim might invoke when he asks himself whether he should, after all, forgive the wrongdoer.

There is a lot to be said for a spirit of "there but for the grace of God" in any conflicts with others, and indeed in our ethical lives as a whole. But as a response to the problem of forgiveness we are discussing it is confused on some crucial points. First, it again comes too close to excusing the wrongdoer, to diminishing his responsibility, to a point where what is going on is better described as sympathetic understanding rather than forgiveness. Instead, I suggest that sympathetic understanding is compatible with a refusal to forgive. Griswold concurs: "The 'common frailty' thesis might just as well lead to the view that it is all the more important – just because we are so frail – to hold ourselves and each other accountable by not forgiving unless there is warrant for doing so" (Griswold 2007: 66).

Second, it would be hard to delimit the scope of such an approach, for it would seem to rule out the possibility of any form of robust condemnation based on the key difference between *me* and *you*: that it is you who are responsible for the offence, not I; but more than that, it was you who committed the offence *against me*. And I am justifiably furious about that. G&M might have a point if they were referring to some idealized imperative that applied to saints; but in so far as I am not a saint, then I take the offence personally and I am offended. It was committed by someone who meant harm to me, or who should have taken greater care to avoid harming me.

Indeed, G&M ask me, the victim, to imagine that I might well have committed the same offence if things had been different. But what if I cannot by any stretch imagine committing that particular offence? This need not be a limitation of my imagination, it might actually be a sign that I do not have any experience of doing *such* nasty things as this. Now, while it is true that any number of adverse situations might surprise me in the future by revealing what I am in fact capable of, the key point here is that there has to be a limit to my imagination: my self-understanding relies on there being certain things I cannot imagine doing, however great the temptation or incentive or provocation. Part of my confidence in these limits is what defines me as a moral individual. No matter how much a reporter offered me for juicy tidbits about my celebrity wife, I cannot – here and now – imagine any sum being great enough for me to betray her in this way (although I abstractly accept that might change in the future). So human solidarity is all very well when it comes to a starving stranger stealing my food, and I can confidently say "there but for the grace"; it is quite another when it comes to a betrayal of trust between intimates, when all the victim can say is "How could he ...?"

Third, it is of course true that if my upbringing had been marked by much greater deprivation, I might be a lot more inclined to commit such an offence; but then it would no longer be *me* against whom the offence was committed. The whole point about me is that I was – completely contingently, of course – not brought up like that. It is now too late to wonder what I would have done or said or thought because it would be a completely different ethical encounter.

This is not to reject G&M's account completely, if it can be taken as an impetus to the deployment of greater imagination and sensitivity in trying to make sense of the wrongdoer's action, to understand the degree of his responsibility; and Griswold would surely agree with this too. But this will come too close to understanding the wrongdoer's action, and thereby excusing or justifying it

– rather than forgiving it. Instead, I would argue that forgiveness becomes a genuine issue precisely when I *cannot* excuse or understand the offence, no matter how hard I try, no matter how hard the wrongdoer repents, because the offence is stubbornly incomprehensible. The starting thought towards forgiveness is not "I see" but rather "How could she ...?" As soon as I say "I see", then it is as if I have already grasped the problem and there is no work left to do. But when I say "How could she ...?", full of pain and anger, and *then* manage to forgive, this is a real accomplishment.

In saying this I have been influenced by an insight from Jacques Derrida, phrased as one of his notorious paradoxes:

> In order to approach now the very concept of forgiveness, logic and common sense agree for once with the paradox: it is necessary, it seems to me, to begin with the fact that, yes, there is the unforgivable. Is it not, in truth, the only thing to forgive? The only thing that *calls* for forgiveness?
> (Derrida 2001: 32, original emphasis)[4]

I do not know about the rest of Derrida's argument, but I think this expresses a profound insight about the failure of conditional accounts. First, we should be clear to understand "unforgivable" *not* as meaning simply "very serious", and I declared at the start that I am not discussing war crimes and genocide. Instead, we are talking about a personal, individual response coloured by bafflement and hurt. For Derrida, the very notion of an offence being in principle forgivable already entails its being forgiven, in some possible world or at some point in the future; so the nominally forgivable offence is nothing more than the first move in another norm-governed transaction like bringing the "gift" for the dinner host. Whether or not the act is then nominally forgiven adds nothing new to our understanding of that act.

Griswold has little time for Derrida (see Griswold 2007: 63 n. 22, 90 n. 52). For Griswold, either an act is forgivable or it is not. Some acts might be genuinely unforgivable, meaning that the act is so serious and/or the perpetrator so unrepentant that nobody's forgiveness would be appropriate in that situation. The only way for Griswold to interpret Derrida is to say that an apparently unforgivable act turned out to be – upon reflection, after the heat of the moment – appropriately forgivable. In other words, there is a truth value to forgivability: in the same way that the offence takes place (or does not take place) at a time t_1, and the wrongdoer's repentance takes place (or does not take place) at time t_2, then the temporally limited package of offence and repentance is either forgivable or not, timelessly. In contrast, Derrida presupposes an open future. The act is unforgivable ... *until it is forgiven*: there is nothing in the offence itself (or in the package of offence and repentance) that contains the subsequent forgiveness, in the sense of the norms of appropriateness. Forgiveness might ensue, or it might not – it is genuinely up to the wrongdoer, acting unpredictably in an open future. And if it does ensue, even if Griswold would applaud the forgiveness as appropriate, this does not then reveal the offence to have been forgivable all along: indeed, the offence may continue to seem to others as unforgivable, but this need not matter in the slightest to the victim.

SELF-FORGIVENESS

In this final section I want to combine aspects of my discussions of apology and of forgiveness. The wrongdoer may feel that apology is not enough, and can never be enough, for what he has done. Even if he has been forgiven by the victim, he may not be able to forgive himself. Indeed, it might seem that the only way he can take responsibility for what he has done is precisely by refusing to forgive himself, and striving continuously and persistently to make up for the harm caused to others. This can be admirable. But in its corrupt form it can be self-indulgent, especially in cases where the harm caused has only been to oneself. In such cases a therapist might try to persuade the person to forgive himself.

The concept of self-forgiveness is inherently suspicious, as if I were waiving away the naggings of my conscience or indeed waiving away the justified grievances of others. The risk is that I can in principle forgive myself for anything. At least in bilateral situations of apology and other-forgiveness, the bilaterality could ground some objective norms of appropriateness, and allow for external challenge. Ultimately, self-forgiveness seems to come too close to smugness and arrogance at best; at worst it could involve ignoring or glossing over episodes which one *ought* to find shameful. Despite these risks, there might be a role for a healthy self-forgiveness that is lucid, informed, impartial and uncompromising when dealing with shameful aspects of one's past. At the very least, self-forgiveness can be seen as more healthy than other approaches to the shameful past, such as sulking or self-denigration which will undermine present capacities to lead one's life. A healthy self-forgiveness might also be part of a larger strategy of relinquishing one's youthful perfectionistic project: one sign of middle age is to accept that although one will never play for the Premier League, or be a millionaire, or be a saint, one can at least be oneself.

Jeffrey Blustein (2000) offers an account of self-forgiveness as a particular kind of taking responsibility. He considers the example of Felicia in William Trevor's novel *Felicia's Journey* (1994), a harrowing tale of an inexperienced young Irish girl who, through bad luck and bad choices, ends up homeless on the streets of an English Midlands town. However, what is remarkable about Felicia is her refusal to disown her past. Blustein comments:

> What is difficult for the reader to understand is how Felicia can value her former inexperienced and credulous self for leading her to where she is when this is such a pitiable state. Yet despite the shabby circumstances of her street life, Felicia ... manages to triumph over adversity by constructing a narrative of her life in which present is linked to and explained by a past she neither endorses nor denies. She does not deny that she played an active part in bringing herself to her abject condition nor does she make excuses for herself. She takes up this part of her past and acknowledges it as her own, and her acknowledging it as her own uplifts her. (Blustein 2000: 2)

Blustein then describes three components of what such "taking responsibility" involves. The first is the "retrospective construction of meaning" (*ibid.*: 8). This is not a metaphysical thesis about backward causality, but rather a statement of how (a) the full meaning of past events may only be revealed in the subsequent events that followed, and about how (b) the meaning of the past changes because of the changing relationships between the past events and the present observers and rememberers. This is a basic truth about understanding and relating the history of a country or a people (indeed, history cannot be done in any other way), but it is also a truth about biographies, my own and other people's. The corollary, of course, is that the meaning may yet change further into the future, in more or less predictable ways. There is room for bias and self-interest in my own interpretations of the past, as there is in my enquiries into the present; but there is also a sense of doing justice to the past, beyond mere coherence with past facts (remembered or documented) and consistency with other people's accounts.

Blustein's second component of taking responsibility is "appropriation" (*ibid.*: 10). This has to do with appropriating the past as *my* past, with decisions made by me rather than a past self, and this helps to link it to the present within the life of a single person. Sometimes the gulf may be too big, as with a war veteran who has been utterly transformed by his recent trauma and therefore cut off from his pre-war self. Sometimes the past may not be intelligible enough for appropriation, as in the case of Agnes the adulterous wife in the previous section. When appropriation is not possible, there is a real risk of fragmentation of identity. Blustein is careful to stress that appropriation is not approbation; one can still condemn the past decision, continue to regret it, and seek to make up for it. Indeed, it is only once I have appropriated the past decision that I have the right to criticize it forcefully, since it has essentially become "my business". With the shameful unappropriated past, the first instinct is just to ignore it as much as possible, and hope it gets forgotten. Blustein also stresses that appropriation is not "living in the past" via escapist reminiscences – instead, the action of appropriation is pulling the past into the present.

The third and final component is "thematization" (*ibid.*: 12). In reflecting on one's past events, one can recognize themes or motifs, one can recognize links between different events in the past and present, and bring things together into a characteristic understanding of a human life. The most obvious themes are personal relationships, but thematization also includes coming to see an event as having instrumental value, as when I judge that it was necessary for me to undergo a difficult episode (failure in a career or marriage) to make me appreciate the subsequent, more fulfilling episode.

At the heart of self-forgiveness is a person who still has a life to lead. It is not about one person (now) forgiving or refusing to forgive another person (then); it is not about a decision that can be made now, and the situation is sorted. It is a decision that has to be made within the context of an ongoing life. Felicia, homeless on the streets of a Midlands city, had plenty of legitimate grievances, against her family, against the men who took advantage of her naïveté, and against cruel fate itself. She could seek a certain amount of solace in that grievance, cling to it, shape her identity around the role of the victim, and tell her story to anyone who would listen. But this would be to remain chained to the past.

Some shame or remorse, or sense of failure, or a sense of having disappointed others, will be so great as to drive a person to suicide. They might even express their suicidal intent in terms of the "responsible" thing to do. But in those cases where, for whatever reason, suicide was *not* chosen, there are stark choices about how to spend the rest of one's life without being undermined by the past. Taking responsibility by self-forgiveness represents a much stronger engagement with the past, and therefore with the future, than taking responsibility by self-acceptance. Self-acceptance is compatible with self-pitying victimhood, with demoting one's bad choices to the status of unlucky external events that befell one. Self-forgiveness recognizes the bad choices for what they are, but integrates them much more intimately into one's ongoing life in the three ways that Blustein discusses.

I have been talking about taking responsibility for one's past. In Chapter 8 I will discuss the related phenomenon of taking responsibility for a *present* situation of adversity, an adversity so apparently permanent as to defeat hope and any thought of enduring through temporary dark times. I will argue that, in the same way as one can embrace one's past mistakes, one can embrace the present situation as well, and in both cases have a real chance of taking control of one's remaining life.

4

PUNISHMENT

The previous chapter, on apologies and forgiveness, essentially concerned the interpersonal aspect of retrospective responsibility. In this chapter I would like to return to the legal context. The state is not in a position to forgive, although it can show mercy – and we will be discussing mercy later on. But above all the state has the power and authority to hold someone responsible by *punishing* them for their crime. That is what this chapter is principally about. Slightly less formally, and with less draconian punishments at its disposal, a profession or a club can punish its members for an infraction of its rules. Even less formally, a teacher can punish her pupils, but this must be justified in terms of the school's educational goals. Finally, and least formally of all, a parent can punish his child. It is important to realize that conceptually, an individual – acting *as* an individual – cannot "punish" another individual, although of course she may blame him, be angry at him, hurt him, take revenge on him, and so on. The concept of punishment presupposes some sort of institutional relationship between the punisher and the punished, where this relationship provides the punisher with the necessary *authority* to impose harsh treatment. (Even a family is an institution in this sense.) In what follows I shall be mainly discussing the criminal law in a modern liberal democratic state, and only occasionally discussing other fora where punishment can be imposed.[1]

Perhaps one paradoxical thing about the criminal law is that, strictly speaking, a crime is not committed against the victim but against the state "through" the victim. The victim can be robbed, bloodied and beaten, and yet the state is concerned with the disruption of the moral order caused by the robbery and the assault. Sometimes the criminal justice system has even proven itself to be quite insensitive to the victim, as is notorious in rape cases. This is what distinguishes criminal law from tort law; for in the latter, it is one individual who complains about the actions of another individual (the alleged "tortfeasor"), and the state's role is to arbitrate by determining the extent of the harm and enforcing compensation. Under the criminal law, it is the state who prosecutes the offender, regardless of what the victim thinks of the matter, and even regardless of whether the victim would prefer the offender to be acquitted. The victim's only role is to help provide details about the crime and the circumstances that might have led to it.

The traditional philosophical problem of punishment is: how can a liberal democratic state justify the infliction of deliberate harm on one of its citizens? A law on theft has been lawfully promulgated and publicized, a citizen freely and knowingly breaks the law for obvious reasons of self-interest, hoping that he will not get caught. Nevertheless, he is caught and tried in a court. Evidence is presented; the court finds him guilty, and sentences him to be punished. Why exactly? This is a trickier question than it looks. The first answer is: because he was responsible for breaking a rule, an event in the past. And now he is sentenced to a year in prison, an event in the future: he is to be punished *for* the theft. But how is the past theft linked to the future incarceration, how is the state justified in deliberately harming the criminal because of the theft?

In this chapter I will begin by outlining the two traditional answers to the problem; then I will consider Jean Hampton's "moral education theory" of punishment, which seeks to avoid the problems which the two traditional answers encountered. Following on from Hampton's theory, I will then argue that the traditional problem of justifying punishment has been misconceived. Finally, I will consider the practice of cancelling just punishment through mercy, pardons and amnesties.

CONSEQUENTIALISM AND RETRIBUTIVISM

There have traditionally been two kinds of answer to the problem of justifying punishment, the *consequentialist* and the *retributivist*, and each of these theories admits of different versions.

The consequentialist response to the crime

The consequentialist answer justifies the harm by reference to the desirable consequences, both for society and for the individual himself. In its simplest form, this is achieved by *deterrence*: the widely known existence of punishment (the knowledge that the state carries out its threats to punish, and that prison is not a nice place) deters the tempted, and deters this particular offender from re-offending after his punishment. As a result there is a lower crime rate, and greater order in society. Since punishment is expensive for the state, there is a further question about the nature and duration of the punishment for a given crime in order to get the maximum deterrent effect for the smallest outlay, but this is no longer a question for philosophers but one for penologists, who regularly suggest adjustments to the types and durations and structures of punishment.

As we saw in the objections to strict liability, the main objection to the deterrence account is that it seems to involve *using* the individual criminal as a means to desirable social consequences. Once the desirable ends have been defined, then the state can resort to "whatever works" to achieve those consequences at minimum cost. Nothing is ruled out in principle. And this means, for example, that the same deterrent effect can be achieved by framing a random individual as by spending far greater public resources, perhaps without success, to catch the genuine culprit. The framing of the Birmingham Six is a case in point. In 1974, two Birmingham pubs were destroyed by separate bombs, exploding within minutes of each other, and killing twenty-one people. The police were unable to find the bombers, so they fabricated evidence against six Irishmen who happened to be in the area at the time. The fabrication was only discovered accidentally in 1991, and the six Irishmen were released and compensated. The consequentialist theory of punishment cannot rule out such fabrication, as long as it is successful. The British public was understandably anxious after the bombings, and the trial of the six Irishmen gave the appearance of an effective police force and a strong deterrent against potential future bombers. (Of course, if the fabrication is discovered, this reduces the consequentialist value of the fabrication somewhat, since the necessary trust in the police is then undermined. But the risk of exposure can be included in the original risk–benefit calculations, so that the fabrication could still be later defended as the best, though not infallible, consequentialist course of action available at the time.)

The consequentialist theory also cannot rule out disproportionality between crime and punishment, nor can it rule out "cruel and unusual punishment".[2] Intuitively we would expect the punishment for graffiti to be proportionately less than the punishment for murder. But under the mantra of "whatever works", it might turn out that only draconian penalties (in length and barbarity) can effectively deter certain kinds of graffiti artists. The consequentialist could not in principle object to public pillories and whippings, to dismemberment for thieves, or to the sexual humiliation of Iraqi war prisoners by the American army at Abu Ghraib in 2004.

The simplest form of consequentialist theory involves deterrence. Another form involves rehabilitation, and this is sometimes dressed up in a full "rehabilitationist" theory. The two forms of consequentialism differ in the way they understand the criminal. The deterrence theory treats the potential criminal essentially as a rational *gambler*, someone who makes risk–benefit calculations about whether to steal the television or not, and the state wants to influence those calculations by increasing the apparent risk (more police) and increasing the apparent cost (harsher sentences) that the individual would incur when the gamble fails. The rehabilitationist theory, on the other hand, treats the potential criminal as essentially *ill*, someone who is constitutionally unable to perceive the correct values which the law defends. As such he merits not punishment so much as treatment, to restore him to a healthy law-abiding state. One advantage with this approach over the deterrence approach is that it is also interested in the *causes* of the "illness", such things as socio-economic deprivation, poor state education, lack of social workers and of support for families, and so on. As such it promotes greater integration between the judicial system and the social welfare system. Rehabilitationists usually argue that crime is often the result of a failure in social welfare provision, and therefore the response to crime should not be "hard" treatment but rather the "soft" reinforcement and refinancing of social support and facilities.

However, like the deterrence account, the rehabilitationist account comes too close to a "whatever works" approach, and could not in principle rule out psychologically traumatic "cures" such as those made notorious by the film *Clockwork Orange*. In that film, the criminal is forced to watch scenes of violence after being injected with a nauseous drug, the idea being that future temptations to crime will evoke, in the manner of Pavlov's dog, the same deterrent nausea. As such, the treatment meted out by the rehabilitationist is better described as reprogramming or conditioning, something that falls far short of the respect for autonomy that characterizes normal attempts to persuade.

The retributivist response to the crime

The response begins with the obvious answer: the state should punish the individual when it can be proven beyond reasonable doubt that she has freely and knowingly committed a crime, and is therefore morally responsible – full stop. For the consequentialist, the link between crime and punishment is *contingent*; it is one event followed by another event, without any necessary linkage between the two. If a "punishment" can achieve the same deterrent effect by fabrication, then so be it. For the retributivist, thinking about the crime essentially involves thinking about the punishment, and the punishment expresses the direct recognition of the offender's responsibility. So fundamental is this conceptual link that a five-year-old child can understand it.[3]

There are two popular metaphors, neither of them very good, to explain the link between the crime and the punishment. According to the first, the criminal disrupts the moral equilibrium of society, and only her punishment will restore that equilibrium. But this raises awkward metaphysical questions about what exactly this equilibrium is, and who ascertains its disruption, and how the punishment is supposed to restore it. Even in cases where the punishment matched the crime precisely, it is still disingenuous to speak of any cancellation of the crime in irreversible cases. No amount of punishment will bring the murder victim back to life, nor will it remove the murderer's status as a murderer. According to the second metaphor, the criminal has attempted to gain an unfair advantage by not playing according to the rules, and thereby incurs a debt to society; the punishment is the payment of the debt. This metaphor might work in the case of theft; but if punishment were no more than the payment of a debt, then this would be achieved by returning the money to the rightful owner, without any *further* need for incarceration or community service. And the debt metaphor seems to fall apart completely in cases of murder, assault or rape. Instead of these two metaphors, I think it is better to accept the conceptual link between the crime and the punishment as somehow foundational, neither requiring nor offering a further explanation. It is in the very nature of an institutional rule to require penalties for infraction. Whether one invokes one of the metaphors or this foundational status, the retributivist account links the punishment directly to the individual and the crime, and thus prevents the problem of fabrication and the problem of disproportionality.

The retributivist would say that framing the Birmingham Six was wrong *even if* it led to any amount of good consequences. And this sounds plausible. But it becomes more problematic when it works the other way. The retributivist seems committed to saying that the criminal should be punished even if the punishment does *no good at all*, either to the individual or to society.[4] That starts to sound just as vindictive as the draconian punishments which the consequentialist was accused of favouring. Indeed, the retributivist would insist on the punishment even if it made things *worse*, for example by brutalizing the prisoner into a callous determination to re-offend.

Because of the problems with both accounts, modern penal policies usually have some sort of hybrid account, although tilting more to one account or another in different aspects or in different countries. The hybrid policy will usually begin with two clear retributivist constraints against framing the innocent and against disproportionality; within those constraints, the policy can be regularly adjusted along deterrent and rehabilitationist lines. But as with all pragmatic compromises, there is a strong whiff of the *ad hoc*.

Differing views of parole and recidivism

The disagreement between the consequentialist and the retributivist is also revealed in their differing attitudes to two other phenomena: the parole process, and the "three strikes" policy. If a prison sentence is for ten years, say, the prisoner may be eligible for parole after five years, depending on his obedience within the prison and/or his demonstration of sincere repentance. The consequentialist will justify each condition as follows: (a) if there is an incentive for the prisoner to behave well, this will reduce the costs of his punishment; (b) if the prisoner has genuinely repented halfway through the sentence, then the rehabilitation has been achieved and there is no point to keeping him there further. (In the same way, of course, the consequentialist could argue that if the prisoner has not repented at the end of his sentence, and therefore represents a continuing risk to society, then he should be kept in longer.) Either way, the consequentialist will adduce this flexibility as an inherent advantage. The parole system would still need fine-tuning, of course, in case the existence of parole reduces the *pre-crime* deterrence effect of the sentence (i.e. the sentence would not be taken seriously enough by the tempted).

There is a problem with the reliability of the parole officer's judgement that the offender has indeed repented; the offender has every incentive simply to act the part. At this point, however, the philosopher could again step aside and leave the problem to the parole officer or psychologist, someone with experience of working with prisoners. But philosophically, the consequentialist makes a valid point about the possibility of a criminal – especially a first-time criminal – "getting the message" very early on during her prison sentence, and therefore being safe to let out.

The retributivist, on the other hand, has to reject the whole idea of parole in principle. For him, the punishment is linked, purely and simply, to the offender's responsibility for the crime; the greater the responsibility and the more severe the crime, the more severe the punishment, and the prisoner has to serve out its entire length – no more and no less. If there are reasons for leniency, then these should have been heard during the trial phase, and the resulting sentence should have reflected this. And even if the prisoner has learned her lesson, even if she is sincerely repentant halfway through the sentence, she has not yet been fully punished, and so, it is claimed, cannot be repentant to the correct "depth". Indeed, the retributivist believes that the morally healthy individual, feeling genuine and appropriate remorse for her crime, will *want* to serve out her sentence without parole, as if purging the stain from her past. And the converse is also true: even if she has not learned her lesson at all, she still has to be released at the end of her sentence precisely because she has paid her debt, and it would be simply unjust to keep her longer.

The "three strikes" policy is a recent consequentialist response to an evident failure of deterrence. Also known as "habitual offender" or "persistent offender" policies, almost half of US states have them in some form or for some offences, and they remain controversial. The simple version runs as follows: if an offender is caught perpetrating the same offence as on two previous occasions, then the penalties are dramatically increased, far beyond proportionality. Another version will say that two "serious" offences of any kind puts the offender in a position where *any* further offence, including a relatively trivial shoplifting, will result in a lengthy prison term. The idea is that ordinary deterrence has not managed to prevent the first and second attempts, and so a well-publicized warning of a much more serious penalty will deter the third attempt. In addition, if the offender is nevertheless undeterred from the third attempt, then the state is justified in concluding that the offender's behaviour cannot be modified by rational threats of incentives, and he has to be physically isolated from society for the longer term.

Once again the consequentialist is driven by the thought of "whatever works". The retributivist, on the other hand, will always oppose three-strike policies precisely because the third conviction will not result in a punishment of the third *crime* but in the punishment of the *person* for who he is. The paradigm of criminal justice, they continue, involves deliberately ignoring certain things about the defendant: above all his past and his character. All that should be of interest to the court is whether he committed the crime and whether he was morally responsible for committing it. Normally a jury is not informed of the defendant's criminal record precisely because of the fear that it will prejudice them against him.

HAMPTON'S MORAL EDUCATION THEORY OF PUNISHMENT

Jean Hampton's influential article "The Moral Education Theory of Punishment" (1984) argues against both the consequentialist and retributivist theories and in favour of her own moral education theory. Punishment is best justified, she argues, as an attempt by the state not to deter or to seek retribution but to morally educate the offender, and to indirectly educate the rest of society as well. In many cases, she acknowledges, the offender will not be educated, in which case deterrence and restraint must be invoked for the usual consequentialist reasons: but the *guiding ideal* throughout is that the offender will emerge from the process better educated. The goal of such education is not to deter the self-interested gambler but to change his way of thinking about himself, about the crime and about crime in general: the morally educated offender will welcome the punishment as deserved, and will not be tempted to re-offend because he will understand the moral point of the criminal law. At the same time, moral education constitutes a genuine attempt to communicate with and persuade a rational autonomous human being, rather than merely recondition and reprogram him as the rehabilitationist would advocate.

The notion of moral education may sound sinister, since it could imply a homogenous official morality intolerant of pluralism. But the sort of moral principles Hampton has in mind are uncontroversial ideas about justice and community which young children have to learn both at home and through the state schooling system. Trying to communicate with a thief about the wrongness of theft might also be sinister if it were only the criminal justice system delivering the message punitively; but Hampton is clear that the threatened penalties are only one part of the message to the offender and of the response by the state – the other part is a widespread support system for those individuals tempted to commit crime as a result of social deprivation.

While many philosophers discuss punishment directly in terms of the state, and then mention the family as a derivative form, it is important that Hampton stresses the family as the paradigmatic example. The parent will sometimes punish the child via paternalistic terror, and without accompanying explanation: the child simply *must not* do certain things, especially very dangerous or very cruel things. But in less extreme situations the good parent will be concerned not with simply restraining and channelling the child, but with explaining to the child why she ought to do one thing and not another – in other words with morally educating her by engaging her in discussion about moral reasons. Again, there is nothing complicated or sinister about the Golden Rule, for example, and its attempt to get the child to imagine the world from the perspective of another and thereby to come up with her own moral conclusions.

And in line with this broad goal of moral education, the good parent will sometimes need to resort to hard treatment to get the message through. The wrongness of the action can sometimes only be perceived via hard treatment, where the hard treatment is carefully described as *punishment* which the action *deserves* and not, as the child might be tempted to see it, as arbitrary power: the moral sting of the educative rebuke has to be accompanied, says Hampton, by a physical sting or some painful deprivation (of treats or freedoms) and accompanying shaming. By explaining to the child what moral responsibility is in her own person and her own acts, the child learns not only what it is, but how to *take* responsibility for her acts, and how to *become* a responsible person. Here is Hampton:

> Punishments are like electric fences. At the very least they teach a person, via pain, that there is a 'barrier' to the action she wants to do, and so, at the very least, they aim to deter. But because these punishment 'fences' are

marking *moral* boundaries, the pain which these 'fences' administer (or threaten to administer) conveys a larger message to beings who are able to reflect on the reasons for these barriers' existence: they convey that there is a barrier to these actions *because* they are morally wrong.

(Hampton 1984: 212)

The pain is not the message; the pain draws attention to the message, which is a moral message, a message not about an arbitrary arrangement of power but about an objective moral truth. But importantly, the moral message should not be experienced as isolated or idiosyncratic, for it should fit more or less with the general programme of moral education which the child receives, both at home and in other institutional contexts such as the school or the church. If the moral education is successful, the child will grow into a responsible adult who then refuses to do the action even when the fence is no longer there, even when she could confidently get away with it, and even when she would be strongly tempted to do the action for all the familiar self-interested reasons.

Hampton is optimistic that reasons are available for all moral prohibitions that have to be backed up with threats of force. At the very least the parent can appeal to the child's innate sympathy by describing details of her classmate's suffering that might not have been sufficiently evident. Or if one of two children demands more than half the cupcake, the parent should be able to explain, and the child should be able to see, that it would be fair if each got an equal half. Even when the child is not able to fully grasp the parent's explanations with support from the electric fences, Hampton is optimistic that the child will be "primed" by sensitively and consistently enforced domestic punishment to be sensitive to the moral reasons underlying interpersonal relations and her eventual life as an adult citizen. Importantly, the moral reasons given by the parent should be no more than rungs on a ladder, a ladder which is then discarded when one has reached the top: after all, the best reason not to steal is simply "that it would be theft". If the adult has to ask why exactly theft is wrong, then his education is revealed as incomplete.

Hampton's moral education theory might sound a bit too close to the retributivist theory. But although retributivism demands that punishment fit the crime (the offender gets what he deserves), it is not directly concerned with the offender himself. The moral education theory, by contrast, is concerned not only that the offender *understand* why he deserved punishment, but also conceives of the punishment as ultimately *good* for the offender, as morally improving him. The aim is not just to get the offender to accept society's moral norms grudgingly and tentatively, but for him to accept them at a deeper level, where they will establish a stronger bulwark against temptation in his psychic economy. By focusing in this way on the offender rather than on the offence, Hampton claims her theory solves some of the metaphysical problems that bedevilled the pure retributivist account: there is much less that is mysterious in moral education than there is in the idea of punishment cancelling the crime.[5]

Finally, the moral education theory, writes Hampton, can also deal better with the problem of parole than can retributivism. As we saw above, the present parole policy in most judicial systems is justified by consequentialist considerations: parole is offered as an incentive to good behaviour in the prison, as well as a recognition that there may be no point to keeping the offender in prison if he is genuinely repentant. Hampton argues that the moral education theory of punishment would side with retributivism in supporting determinate sentencing (i.e. "five years means five years", with no parole) – but, she argues, it would not come across with the draconian vindictiveness of which retributivism is accused. The point about moral education is that it can only be offered, not enforced. "The fact that parole boards in this country have tried to coerce repentance is, from the standpoint of [the moral education] theorist, a grave and lamentable mistake" (*ibid.*: 232), partly because it invites pretence and manipulation, but mainly because it goes against the whole spirit of educating someone to be a free and autonomous human being. Determinate sentencing is better, continues Hampton, because:

> a criminal's experience of repentance is produced in large part by the expectation of receiving full punishment, so that the state's subsequent failure to inflict it could lead to

a weakening of the criminal's renunciation of the action. Like a bad but repentant child who will conclude, if he is not punished by his parents, that his action must not have been so bad, the repentant criminal might well need to experience his complete sentence in order to 'learn his lesson' effectively.   (*Ibid.*: 234)

The complete sentence allows the criminal to undergo purification and transformation, so that he may truly come to say that his *past* self was the one who did not understand and who committed the crime: it is this distance from the crime, says Hampton, that is the hallmark of moral responsibility. To put it bluntly, the prisoner needs the time; the time to think and to accept his responsibility for the crime, and the time to accept his own *need* for improvement through punishment. Importantly, however, Hampton is not dogmatic about this, because of her practical concern about the possibility of mistaken over-sentencing. If enough evidence were available that the necessary transformation had taken place, the moral education theory would allow a suspension or pardon ("*not* just a parole"; *ibid.*: 235). It is interesting that she has recourse to a pardon rather than to a parole, precisely because of the meanings expressed by both. I will be returning to the subject of pardons later in this chapter.

GETTING THROUGH TO THE OFFENDER

Lord Hewart, in 1924 the Lord Chief Justice of England, said: "It is not merely of some importance, but of fundamental importance that justice should not only be done, but should manifestly be seen to be done."[6] This oft-quoted remark is normally taken as referring to the value, both for the public and for the legal profession, of a thoroughly open system of justice. Only transparency can allow the trust necessary for stable civil society. However, there is a less common reading of this maxim, and that is the importance for the *offender* to understand the charges against her. Hampton says:

the hero seeking revenge in the Western movie, for example, never simply shoots the bad guy in the back when he finds him – he always confronts the bad guy first (usually in the presence of other people) and tells him *why* he is about to die. Indeed, the movie would be unsatisfying if he didn't make that communication.   (Hampton 1984: 216)

However, in a footnote on page 223, Hampton concedes that the death penalty would not be justifiable by the moral education theorist; for death can hardly be a *benefit* to the offender, and in death there is no opportunity for moral education (i.e. in order to return to society).

Sometimes, of course, the message to be communicated by the punishment will not get through, and the offender will see his situation as merely unlucky rather than deserved, and see the judicial system as powerful rather than authoritative. When this happens, Hampton agrees, *punishment* has not really taken place at all precisely because the educative message did not get through and therefore the educative transformation could not take place. And it is only the educative transformation that can retroactively justify the harsh treatment meted out to this particular offender.

Consider an example which I paraphrase from Peter Winch's (1972) article "Ethical Reward and Punishment". Winch asks us to consider three prisoners, who have been sentenced for the "same" crime (the inverted commas are important, as we shall see):

- Prisoner A thinks to himself: "The police are getting much too good; when I get out, I shall go straight."
- Prisoner B thinks to himself: "The police are getting good, so I shall have to be more careful next time. I will make sure to do X, Y, and Z to avoid getting caught."
- Prisoner C thinks to himself: "This prison sentence is no more than I deserve. I now understand that I have done wrong, and will go straight when I get out."

Now, from the point of view of deterrence, there is no difference between A and C: both have been successfully deterred, whereas B has not. But notice that although the outcome of A's and B's thoughts differs, they are actually thinking in the same way: the police and the criminal justice system are merely obstacles, to be more or less successfully negotiated. The only difference between A and B is in the contingencies of their respective calculations, and/ or in their own attitudes to perceived risk. This means that they do not see their respective crimes as in any way morally wrong (whereas they do understand legal prohibitions), and because of that they cannot conceive of their prison sentence as a *punishment for* a moral wrong – in the full sense of the concept of punishment. Their sojourn in the prison is an arbitrary restriction, to be avoided if possible or endured if necessary. It is only prisoner C who sees the prison sojourn as genuine punishment, as a way of taking responsibility for a crime. He committed the crime without fully perceiving the moral import of what he was doing, and it is only now, in being punished *for that crime* that he comes to understand that what he did was a crime in the moral sense. Thinking about the punishment becomes a way of thinking about the crime, for they are conceptually, not contingently, linked. Coming to see oneself as morally responsible for the past crime necessarily entails seeing oneself as deserving punishment in the present, indeed as needing punishment. If we recall my "present perfect" account of responsibility in Chapter 1, I am saying that the crime is still "in" the offender, despite being committed in the past. It doesn't matter when exactly the crime was committed; what matters is his present lack of understanding as revealed by his carrying the unpunished crime with him until now.

But this also means that the act that C thinks about turns out to be different from that which A and B think about, even if the criminal law would define the acts in the same terms. This is because the meaning of an act may be partly indeterminate at the time of performance: the rest of the meaning can only be discovered after the performance, perhaps long after, through recollection, reinterpretation and remorse. Again, this is not changing the *facts* of the past, which are fixed. What changes is the individual's relationship to those facts, and the new role such facts can assume in the offender's life.

So while the consequentialist and rehabilitationist are concerned with managing the criminals to the advantage of society, Hampton's moral education theory is concerned with getting through to the criminal. Winch's prisoners A and B accept "responsibility" only as part of a morally trivial power struggle with the police, and they are temporarily on the losing side. From the point of view of social policy-makers, all this talk about moral education and genuine punishment might be irrelevant if it does not lead to reduction in the crime statistics. But I have been more interested in the offender's possible experience of punishment as taking responsibility for the crime.

The failure to get through: the example of Eichmann

To see the importance of "getting through", consider the unease that many felt in response to the 1961 trial of Adolf Eichmann, most famously documented in Hannah Arendt's book *Eichmann in Jerusalem: A Report on the Banality of Evil* ([1963] 2011). The outcome of the trial, Eichmann's execution, was never in doubt. But it was important for justice to be done and to be seen to be done, both by the world and by Eichmann, just as it was important that Eichmann should not be presented either as a monster or a psychopath or a cartoon villain. Eichmann was allowed a competent defence lawyer, witnesses and evidence had to be presented under the strict rules of due process, and Eichmann had to be allowed to answer the charges.

What was most striking to Arendt, and which warranted the book's sub-title, was the sheer banality of Eichmann's life, and the terrible way that the banal lives of so many Nazi bureaucrats had been channelled into a ruthlessly efficient killing machine. But equally shocking was Eichmann's sheer moral obtuseness, even as he mounted the scaffold. He was not a stupid man, and he respected conventional morality in most of his personal life and his life after the war. And yet when presented with a veritable mountain of evidence and testimony to support the prosecution case – evidence which he did not dispute – he shrugged his shoulders and effectively said, "I lost the war, you won it; go ahead and kill me." He accepted the outcome of the trial as a matter of revenge or "victor's justice", not punishment. He was being held responsible, he thought, not for his so-called crimes but merely for being on the losing side, and for the mistake of allowing himself to get caught. He was not resentful of his captors and executioners, for he accepted their power to do with him as they pleased, in the same way that he was authorized to process his victims when he was on the winning side.

There are few who would disagree that if anybody deserved to die, it was Eichmann. But I want to suggest that there is a real sense in which he died unpunished, despite the rigour and process of the trial. To Eichmann, his execution was merely the outcome of the same Darwinian forces that had justified his own zealous efforts during the war. It is unlikely the Jerusalem court could have done anything more than they did; and certainly there would be few others who would not have seen justice as having been done. But it is curious and unsettling that a single person – the offender himself – can hold the whole justice system to ransom by refusing to accept its conclusions, and without allowing his opinions to be discredited as the ravings of a lunatic or monster.

Of course, it was probably too big a task for Eichmann to understand the moral reality of what he had done. After all, he had managed to organize the mass Jewish deportations for several years only by building up an elaborate edifice of selective attention, redescription, justification and self-deception, and such an edifice was not going to be brought down by a civilized courtroom, no matter how traumatic the testimony. The only acceptable evidence of the beginnings of awareness by Eichmann would have been a swift descent into madness or a determined intention to commit suicide – although the latter would have been hard to distinguish from an attempt to cheat the hangman.[7]

Mercy

This chapter has been about punishment, about the point of it, and about the offender's understanding of it. Normally a defendant is found guilty and then punished; or he is found innocent and then acquitted. But there is a third option: the defendant is found guilty, but shown mercy, and it is this concept I want to look at in this section. There are two important things to recognize about mercy. First, we have to distinguish mercy from forgiveness. Forgiveness (discussed in Chapter 3) is essentially *interpersonal*: for only the victim (or a close relative of the victim) can forgive the wrongdoer. Mercy, like punishment, is primarily an *institutional* response (i.e. something that only someone with the relevant authority can grant: a president, a judge, a disciplinary tribunal, or even God). The victim's desire or refusal to forgive the offender is irrelevant to whether mercy is to be shown.

Second, mercy is essentially *unjust* in the sense that it enters the picture after all relevant considerations of justice have been aired. It is definitely not the same as justified leniency. During the trial, the judge considers not only whether the defendant did it, and whether he was morally responsible for doing it; she also considers any aggravating circumstances (e.g. the defendant was carrying a gun during the burglary) or any mitigating circumstances (e.g. the various excuses we discussed in Chapter 1), and these will be part of the trial process and will influence the judgment. Nor is mercy the same as *equity* – the process of applying general principles to a particular case in all its complexity, and thereby compromising on some of the principles. For equity is also part of the trial process. In theory, the judgment is the final word of justice, and includes mitigation and equity. So because mercy opposes the final judgment, it is essentially unjust. If mercy is shown, it cannot be on the grounds of the same mitigating circumstances and excuses that have already been considered. Indeed, mercy could also be called unjust in the sense of being unfairly vulnerable to luck. Fairness has to do with treating like cases alike. But the highly individual nature of the granting of mercy suggests an illegitimate role for luck in the proceedings. If two crimes and two offenders are identical in every respect, it is possible that one receives mercy and the other not, depending on the political forces at play in that region or in respect to that crime.

So how can the practice of showing mercy be justified? Here is one consequentialist way. While the justice system is focused on the moral aspects of the offender and his offence, mercy could be granted with a view to certain relevant *non-moral* aspects of the offender, for example his physical or mental health. If the offender was seriously ill or dying at the time of the sentencing, or if he was suffering psychologically because of a recent bereavement, then punishment might be at best pointless and at worst vindictive, especially since if released he would no longer pose a threat to society. The offender could be judged to be "suffering enough" from his illness or the bereavement. These were the grounds for the mercy shown to the "Lockerbie bomber" in 2009.[8]

Another consequentialist way of justifying mercy is to adopt a wider perspective, by looking at the inevitable impact of the punishment on third parties, especially the offender's dependants. The court is supposed to be only interested in the moral responsibility of the individual; but if the offender is the sole breadwinner of a family, her dependants will suffer for as long as she is in prison, and the law will effectively be punishing *them* for something they did not do. As such the eventual mercy is shown not so much to the offender but indirectly to the dependants. However, this solution to the dependants' plight is itself a bit odd. For there is nothing to prevent the offender, once released on mercy, from absconding and leaving the family in the same position. If the court was seriously concerned about the family's welfare, then it could recommend additional direct payments and support from the state's welfare system.

In his important systematic treatment of the subject, John Tasioulas (2003) accommodates justice and mercy within a "communicative theory" of retributivism, itself similar to Hampton's moral education theory above. However, Tasioulas distinguishes between *grievance* retributivism, according to which punishment is deserved for wrongful conduct, and *character* retributivism, where just deserts depend not only on the offender's conduct but also on his underlying moral character (*ibid.*: 116). For the judge to enquire into the offender's character means, for example, to examine his particular background and childhood upbringing. Grievance retributivism, which can accommodate excuses, cannot properly accommodate the effects of the offender's deficient upbringing because of the difficulty of establishing causality, that is, it is hard to say that the upbringing caused this particular offence. Tasioulas puts it eloquently:

> The morally debilitating effects of grinding poverty, severe emotional deprivation, physical abuse and other such

109

evils in one's life do not necessarily alter the fact or level of culpable wrongdoing, nor do they necessarily have the more radical effect of diminishing the offender's status as a moral agent responsible for their actions. But a humanitarian sentiment of "There but for the grace of God go I" may demand that these obstacles to good character be taken into account by tempering the strict requirements of retributive justice.   (*Ibid.*: 116)

This line of reasoning assumes a particular structure of the self, according to which the offender is only responsible for the conduct in a superficial way. Given the deeper structures of his self, produced by an upbringing for which he was not responsible, his choices were constricted at the superficial level, and it is the institution of mercy that can recognize this and respond to it appropriately.

But there are risks with such an approach. Tasioulas's argument is similar to one offered by Martha Nussbaum (1993), and Nussbaum was criticized by Christopher Bennett (2004). Here the disagreement was about a form of mercy relevant to interpersonal relations. Bennett suggests that there is a "good side" and a "bad side" to mercy, and that Nussbaum has focused too much attention on the good side by seeing an unfortunate personal history as clear grounds for mitigating blame. Bennett takes the example of "Grandfather", an elderly racist in Britain (*ibid.*: 5). While Bennett can condemn the racism itself, and would not tolerate it in someone of his own (younger) generation, he can understand the temptation to soften his stance towards Grandfather, given the acquisition of his racist views at a time of widespread casual racism. "There *is* something morally attractive about softening one's condemnation on this basis: it shows understanding, an awareness of how characters are formed; and it recognizes that there are limits to responsibility" (*ibid.*).

But there is a "bad side" as well, for the above temptation involves an assumption that Grandfather is not fully responsible for his present views, and that he could not have been expected to recognize for himself, against his uncritically inherited prejudice, that all races are equal. And yet, asks Bennett, why should we think this, if we are not prepared to condescend or pity Grandfather in other contexts? For it is also a fact that not every person of that generation was racist, or remained racist – it was not as if an entire generation suffered mass hypnosis. In contrast, when Bennett is prepared to remonstrate with a racist of his own generation, he is effectively paying a "back-handed compliment" by implying that the young racist is fully responsible for his views and an appropriate object for attempts to persuade – the young racist is worth criticizing, whereas Grandfather can effectively be indulged and ignored.

Bennett makes a valid point about the potential of mercy to condescend, and the invocation of mercy in interpersonal relations will always be a delicate matter. I am not sure if Grandfather himself would necessarily interpret Bennett's reticence as condescending, however – he might knowingly participate in the same "agreement to disagree" as Bennett himself, precisely in order to preserve friendly relations on other matters. More importantly, I think Bennett is mistaken about the nature of racism, and about the acquisition and loss of racist beliefs. Racism is not an empirical matter that can be settled by evidence; it is a metaphysical matter. Back in the days of slavery, every slave-owner would acknowledge that certain of his slaves would be more intelligent than many whites, but this empirical property did not for a moment grant the slave equal moral status. White children would genuinely love their black nanny as a moral equal, until they reached the age when they adopted their parents' beliefs that the nanny was in fact an inferior, however lovable. In other words, losing one's racist beliefs is not simply a matter of opening one's eyes to an empirical "fact" that all races are equal. Similarly, it is not as if Grandfather knowingly turned away from the empirical evidence in order to protect his racist beliefs. Losing one's racist beliefs is a deeply mysterious process, akin to a religious conversion: something for which there is no formula, and no persuasion.

The other problem with Bennett using racism as an example is that usually racism is an isolated part of a person's character, one that can effectively be ignored while still liking and admiring the rest of the person. But ignoring it is not the same as forgiving it, or showing mercy on it. Nussbaum's original example was of the character Steerforth from Charles Dickens's novel *David Copper-field*. Here the point was that Steerforth's villainy encompassed his entire character, and so could not be isolated or ignored. Of course one could just ignore or avoid Steerforth, but if one is "stuck" with him in close quarters (if he is one's brother, or one's work colleague), or if one comes to like him for any reason, then one will be faced with the problem of trying to understand him. And this will inevitably bring his unfortunate personal history into play. I think Nussbaum's point is one about merciful *understanding* rather than mercy, which is perfectly compatible with a robust condemnation of Steerforth's particular acts of villainy; she is not suggesting that he be held less responsible, or that condemnation of the acts be tempered.

5
MORAL LUCK

At several points in the book so far we have run into the problem of moral luck, and now it is time to face it squarely. The term itself was invented by Bernard Williams in a classic 1975 paper, "Moral Luck", to which Thomas Nagel responded in a paper by the same name. (I will be citing from the revised Williams paper in his 1981 anthology *Moral Luck* (1981a) and from Nagel's revised version in his 1979 anthology *Mortal Questions*.[1])

Both papers begin with the widespread assumption among moral philosophers, lawyers and the general public that morality is – and should be – *immune to luck*. This perceived immunity has deep Christian and Platonic roots, but received its most systematic philosophical elaboration in Kant's moral theory. According to this "Kantian conception" (as Williams calls it), if the agent's intentions are good, or at least not bad, and she has taken all the care and precautions required by the situation (that is, she is not reckless or negligent), then she cannot be held morally responsible for any bad effects that arise from bad luck alone. Indeed, it works both ways: she cannot claim responsibility for positive outcomes arising from good luck. To keep the discussion tidy, I am going to stick to bad luck, as did Williams and Nagel.

The proviso about care and precautions is important: Kant is certainly not saying that good intentions alone can avoid the road

to hell. But if the agent knows and has done all that can reasonably be expected in the situation, then she is not to blame for anything untoward that she unwittingly causes. The agent might feel
bad, of course, as she would whenever bad luck occurs. But the
mere fact that it was caused accidentally by her does not distinguish it morally from any piece of bad luck, elsewhere in the world,
to which she was causally unrelated. It is as if the bad luck merely
happened through her body. This immunity corresponds to the
ideal of the perfectly reasonable and non-negligent agent, who will
never regret any decision: she will always be able to say that she
did what appeared best, given the evidence available at the time,
even if it turned out badly. She regrets the way things turned out,
in the sense that she wishes they had turned out better, but she
cannot coherently regret choosing one option over the other since
she remains confident that she made the best decision given her
knowledge of the situation and of the likely future consequences of
the available options.

Most important for Kant is the fact that *any* rationally competent individual can choose to avoid intending evil, and choose to
take the requisite care and precautions. Of course we are all vulnerable to the vicissitudes of fortune in any number of ways, but
none of these will undermine the moral quality of one's act or one's
will. The expression "moral luck" is thus meant to be an oxymoron.
However, Williams and Nagel want to show that luck does creep
into many ordinary situations to a point that our moral judgements
are affected – not just our spontaneous moral judgements, but our
considered judgements too – and indeed, that our moral lives as
agents and as respondents would be unrecognizable if we lived
them under the strict Kantian conception. In other words, moral
luck is a reality, and this opens up some real paradoxes.

In terms of focus, Williams is generally interested in the agent's
assessment of herself; Nagel is more interested in the assessment
of others, including the legal system. Let me start by introducing
Nagel's useful taxonomy here (1979: 28), so that it is clearer what
we are talking about. There are four types of moral luck:

- *Constitutive luck* has to do with the past, and refers to those
  aspects of one's present character, outlook and being that

114

one was lucky or unlucky to have been born with or that one developed in early childhood. Clearly one had no control over the inheritance or development of such character traits, and therefore one is not responsible for them. And yet we make moral judgements about people's characters all the time. It is true that as adults we have some indirect control over the development of our characters, and so can properly be held responsible for our bad moral traits. But this will only ever be true to a certain extent, and even the persistence, humility and confidence needed for self-improvement might themselves be a product of a lucky upbringing.

- *Situational* or *circumstantial luck* has to do with the present, and refers to the luck of whether or not one finds oneself in a particular situation of adversity that reveals the good or bad aspects of one's character, or that forces uncomfortable dilemmas where one will do wrong whichever way one chooses. Consider two Frenchmen of similar character and background: one manages to get out in June 1940, and the other is trapped in Nazi-occupied France for the duration of the war. The latter faces much more insidious moral dilemmas, on a daily basis, about the extent of his collaboration.[2] But this type of luck is not only about situations that are good or bad in general ways; it is also about particular kinds of good or bad situation that bring out the best or worst in particular types of people. So a budding politician might be courageous in the House of Commons, but might be unlucky enough to be revealed as a physical coward in a bar-room altercation.

- Nagel's third and fourth category mirror each other as the *causes* and *effects of action*. The causes of action have to do with the luck underlying the configuration of different kinds of forces – metaphysical, physical, biological, psychological – that might have contributed to the agent's apparently free action, and indeed to the formation of the agent's intentions and motivations. As Nagel says, in so far as this is not merely an extension of constitutive luck, it basically amounts to the question of free will and determinism. In the introductory chapter I said that I wanted to avoid the free will debate in this book, and so I, like Nagel, will not discuss this category further.

115

- The effects of action have to do with the future, and involve *resultant* or *outcome luck*. Whether we succeed or fail at any endeavour often has a lot to do with luck. Two agents, with exactly the same mindsets (beliefs, desires and intentions), might end up causing morally different outcomes because of factors entirely out of their control. Nagel mentions at least three classes of examples here: (a) intentions thwarted by flukes, as when a bird flies in the path of a bullet, and thereby reduces the agent's crime from murder to a far less serious attempted murder; (b) negligence and recklessness, as in the case where only one of two drunk drivers is charged with man-slaughter after hitting a pedestrian who strayed into his path; (c) decisions made under uncertainty, particularly in politics, as when Chamberlain's signature on the Munich Agreement in 1938 *turned out* to be much worse than he believed at the time, precisely because of what Hitler went on to do.

So ordinary life turns out to be vulnerable to luck in all sorts of ways. Surely this should threaten the confidence with which we hold people responsible for their actions? The Kantian and the determinist will have relatively straightforward solutions to the problem of moral luck: both will say that our ordinary language and our spontaneous emotional responses are simply misleading and misguided, and that in the name of fairness we should do the best we can to ignore the stubborn pervasiveness of luck. However, throughout this book, I have been taking ordinary language, ordinary concepts and ordinary emotional responses very seriously, and so I (along with Nagel and Williams) have to deal with the glaring problem that remains. In the following three sections I want to discuss the first, second and fourth of Nagel's categories further.

CONSTITUTIVE LUCK

When I think about who I am, I am struck by two things: first, the *massive* amount of brute contingency involved in bringing me from non-existence (when there was no "me") to where I am now. It is about (a) the contingency of my parents meeting, (b) the contingency of one particular egg (out of hundreds) being fertilized by one particular sperm (out of hundreds of millions), and (c) the fertilization taking place in one of a near-infinite number of combinations of the two genomes; but it is also about (d) my parents' respective parents meeting, about their grandparents meeting, and so on, each time with exponentially greater improbability back through the family tree. But (e) it is also about the sheer range of random situations and encounters that I went through in childhood, some remembered, some presumed, but the vast majority of them forgotten and of uncertain influence. (When I think of how quickly other animals physically grow from birth to full adult size, when I think of how quickly after birth the giraffe has to learn to run, I am struck by how enormously long it takes us humans to reach our adult form, and therefore how vulnerable we are to all sorts of influences during this period.) And then (f) it is also about the complex, unpredictable and unverifiable effects of my increasingly autonomous decisions and strivings on my developing character itself.

It is hard to imagine how I could possibly be held responsible for *any* of this, and how my character could not be my destiny. And yet when I respond with anger that is inappropriate to the situation, or when I fail to notice what I ought to have noticed, or when I reveal myself to be stingy or cowardly or lazy, then I am subject to blame – and legitimate blame – by both victim and observers: I should have known better, or I should have controlled myself, or I should have paid attention, or I should have made more of an effort, and so on. All these thoughts by victims and observers assume that I am responsible in some way for my character traits, for my emotional responses, for my insensitivities.

Now, I have already discussed some of this problem in the section on responsibility for character (Chapter 2, § "Responsibility for character"), so I want to make a different point about identity here. Daniel Statman (1993: 12) asks us to consider the statement "How lucky I am to have such parents!" The implication is that I am lucky I have *these* parents – rather than any other couple. But any other couple would not have had *me* as a child, they would have had someone else. So once I am in the world, then this man and this woman are necessarily my (biological) parents, and because of this necessity there is nothing lucky or unlucky about that. It was a matter of luck that they met, that they produced me rather than any number of other babies they could have produced, but as soon as I have become a fact of the world, then this "erases" the alternative children who might have come into existence instead of me, leaving only me. As such, the statement "how lucky I am" is not actually true. If, on the other hand, we consider the statement "How lucky that my parents were so *good* to me" or "How lucky that I have always got along so well with my parents," this makes more sense because it might have been logically possible for my parents to have treated me worse or for us not to get along. So in terms of relational identity there is no luck, and in terms of substantive identity there is still plenty of room for luck.

But is there? Pause for a moment and ask *who* is making the judgement that "My parents were so good to me". I am. And here is the point: it is partly *because* my parents were so good to me that I became the person – here and now, many years after my childhood – that I am. If my parents had regularly abused me, say, I would almost certainly not have anything like the self-confidence I do in fact have. As such, we can argue in reverse that *in so far* as my parents were hugely causally responsible for building my self-confidence, and in so far as my self-confidence is an important part of me, then had my parents abused me, the resulting adult many years later *would not be me*. What this means is that, from the perspective of my adult self, here and now, it is too late for me to look back at certain parts of my identity and meaningfully speculate about what might have been. This is not a point about the limits of my imagination: this is a point about the limits of *me*. At this point in time, the self-confidence instilled in me by my parents (among other influences) is a *necessary* part of me, and therefore not – or no longer – a matter of luck. For me to be me, the past could not have been significantly different in this respect.[3]

We have to be careful here, however, not only because the whole notion of causal influence on character development is enormously complicated, but also because the whole question of which properties are important or essential to my identity is also complicated. There is an awful lot to be said here by psychologists, paediatricians and educationalists. One can plausibly say, for example, that one's gender, ethnicity and linguistic culture are an essential part of one's identity, whereas one's hair colour is not. (And if hair colour *is* an essential part, then a biographical-causal explanation is owed about why it is.) But the general point is that the past, when viewed from the present, has *become* less vulnerable to luck in virtue of the particular place in time of my present existence, as later than the past.

A more extreme version of the point I am making can be seen in so-called "wrongful life" suits. The typical pattern of such suits is as follows. A child is born with a severe disability. The disability was the probable outcome of a genetic condition in the child that could have been diagnosed while the child was still *in utero*, or that could have been diagnosed in either of the parents before conception. Either way, if such a condition had been diagnosed, then the woman would have had the option to avoid pregnancy, or to seek a legal abortion. Instead, the woman remained ignorant and gave birth to the child with the disability. The disability, as predicted, turns out to be costly: not only in terms of the money, time and effort required to care for the child, but also in terms of the suffering of the child himself. In a wrongful life suit, the child (represented by the parents) accuses the doctor or hospital of negligence, and demands financial compensation for the ongoing care costs and for the suffering associated with living with such a condition, costs that would not have accrued to the parents if they had avoided the pregnancy or aborted the foetus.[4] The paradox is that the child is arguing that he should not have been allowed to come into existence, but the child is only in the position to *make* the argument once he does exist. And once he exists, it is also too late to curse the bad luck of being born with such a condition. Given that the only alternative was non-existence, then the fact that he exists means that his condition is necessary. Although successful in a controversial Californian case,[5] wrongful life suits have been rejected by most other jurisdictions.

So we reach a position where at least some of the essential elements of my character are not contingent but necessary. However, does this position really help us understand the problem of responsibility? After all, whether something is contingent or necessary, it still seems out of my control – and therefore it would still seem to be inappropriate to be held responsible for it. If it is necessary that I am black, then it makes no sense to blame me for being black when there is nothing I can do about it. However, what this discussion is pointing to is a different understanding of responsibility, one associated with *identity* rather than control. To explain this, imagine a woman, Kathryn, who is passionate about directing films. Perhaps she always knew she wanted to become a director, perhaps she stumbled into it by accident as an adult. Either way, Kathryn[6] has come to care so much about film-making that she identities with it. This is not only a matter of introducing herself to strangers as a director, but it also involves a special attachment to the films she makes, a special vulnerability to criticism of those films, a special concern for good or bad developments in the film world, a passionately engaged perspective in discussions about films with friends, colleagues and journalists. By the time Kathryn has been at this a few years, I want to say that film-making now runs so deep in her life that it has become a necessary part of her identity – in the sense that if she had not developed this particular passion, she would be a different person. In one sense her film-making *is* still in her control, since nobody is forcing her to continue making films; but she identifies with the role so much that she would never – could never – give it up while she was still physically and financially able to continue.[7]

Now, here is the point. Precisely because she identifies with her role of film-maker means that she is willing to take responsibility for the content of that role. When she makes a film, she takes responsibility for it in the sense of being willing to take criticism for it, and to take the trouble to respond to some of the critics. She offers the film as an extension of herself, so that effectively a criticism of the film is a criticism of her. She expects to be held responsible for the film, and for her film-making skills: that is part of what it means to make films. So even if her film-making is a necessary aspect of her identity and therefore no longer a matter of luck (in the sense that a non-film-making alternative reality would not contain *her*), and even if it is not in her control (in the sense that she would never choose to abandon it), it is nevertheless something that she can be held responsible for.

This exploration of identity, luck, roles and responsibility sets up a discussion that I will resume in the second part of this book. For the moment, I want to return to our examination of Nagel's four categories of moral luck.

SITUATIONAL LUCK

Recall the example of the two Frenchmen, the first who emigrated in 1940, and the second who was trapped under the Nazi occupation, there to find himself in situations requiring various degrees of knowing collaboration with evil. Paradoxically, the second Frenchman could also be considered lucky in the sense of having more opportunities for great heroism in the Resistance. But in parallel to this general point about situations, there is also the relational point that an individual may be lucky or unlucky in facing a situation that brought out the best or worst *in him*, given the determinate strengths and weaknesses of his particular character (my example was of a courageous MP whose physical cowardice was exposed in a bar brawl).

In what follows I am going to focus on negative examples, for the sake of simplicity. In addition, while it is fairly easy for another person to live with a hero without envy, it is much more difficult to live with a Nazi collaborator without judging him. Collaboration traumatized a generation of French people, while the British are lucky enough to still remember the Second World War in their simplistic black-and-white terms. Because of the transformative power of action, the collaboration has made the second Frenchman a collaborator, and no matter how often the émigré withholds judgement and asks himself the question "What would I have done?", the fact remains that the collaborator seems to be permanently tainted in a way that the émigré is not.

The bad situation is not mere adversity, like an earthquake or a burst pipe; it is the particularly insidious kind of adversity which places upon me a moral dilemma and thereby forces me to do wrong whichever way I choose. In doing wrong, intentionally, the second Frenchman cannot avoid being responsible for the wrong he does. And even if the costs of non-compliance would have been unreasonably great, perhaps including death, the fact is that he was always sufficiently free to refuse the next degree of collaboration and therefore the Control condition for the paradigmatic kind of moral responsibility is fulfilled. Meanwhile, the émigré Frenchman is off the hook.

One way out of the patent unfairness might be available to the religious believer, and it is philosophically useful to consider this because of the light it throws on the nature of character. An omniscient god would mete out perfect justice in the afterworld, and would judge strictly by character, not by the actions that happened to be "pulled out" of the agent by a lucky or unlucky situation. While divine justice is usually offered as a warning to those able to evade earthly justice, it could also be offered to those who feel hard done by situational moral luck: the hope is that God would be able to judge the person not by his collaboration with the Nazis, but by what he *would have done* in myriad different counterfactual situations. The person's character and identity, and therefore their moral desert, would be bound up in the sum total of all hypothetical behaviour, regardless of the situations they happened to encounter in their real lives. Imagine, then, that the émigré Frenchman soon died after arriving in London. And yet, *ex hypothesi*, he has the same character as the Frenchman who stayed behind and went on to collaborate. Now, even if God can hold the dead émigré responsible, it is not at all clear *what* He is holding him responsible for: not for the collaboration that he would have engaged in had he stayed, and not even for any decision to collaborate he would have made. The émigré, arriving in heaven, would feel understandably aggrieved to be accused of something that he merely would have done. And it would not work the other way for similar reasons: if God managed to judge that the collaborator had a fairly ordinary set of dispositions and therefore did not deserve the opprobrium that by luck his émigré colleague avoided, this would still not remove the stain of his freely chosen collaboration.

There is an interesting overlap between situational moral luck and constitutional moral luck. At the beginning of this chapter I described the former as essentially involved with the present, and the latter as involved with the past. But of course, as I have said before, the past is in the present, and the present becomes the past. If we return to the original example, with the émigré and the collaborator both surviving the war, the problem of situational moral luck during the Nazi period becomes less and less relevant as the émigré and the collaborator age far beyond it. The collaborator (now an ex-collaborator) continues to live in France, into the 1950s and 60s and 70s, and his past collaboration leads to certain important things in his life: perhaps a trial and a prison sentence, perhaps uncomfortable questions from his children, perhaps blackmail from former collaborator colleagues needing money.

Here's the point: the longer the ex-collaborator lives past the events of his collaboration, the more the collaboration affects his life, and the more *necessary* it becomes in the making of who he ends up being. By the time he reaches the 1980s, the collaboration is forty years into the past, and the alternative paths he might have taken from 1940 onwards become less and less easy to imagine – not only that, the hypothetical people who would have resulted, forty years later, from different post-1940 paths become more and more different from the ex-collaborator, and it becomes less and less possible to say that *he* – the ex-collaborator, here and now in the 1980s – should not have started collaborating in 1940. The longer he goes on, the less he is able to say, "I was unlucky to be stuck in France in 1940" since his long-ago collaboration has become a necessary part of his particular present perspective.

The epistemic argument

The above line of thinking is part of a solution to the problem of moral situational luck (and indeed to resultant luck, as we shall see below) called the epistemic argument, developed by Norvin Richards, among others (see Richards 1993). The essential thought is this. Nagel's examples are too stipulative: he stipulates that the two Frenchmen have the same character, and that the émigré would have collaborated just as much as the real collaborator. But in ordinary life the only epistemic access we have to another's character is *through his actions*. Indeed, very often the only epistemic access we have to our *own* character is through the actions that we, perhaps surprisingly, end up performing in the situations we encounter. We might say that in 1940 the two Frenchmen behaved in very similar ways in response to certain shared situations, and we might say they had a similar family and socio-economic background; but after 1940 they no longer shared the same situation. All that we have left is *wild* speculation, completely unjustified by the evidence, or by any testimony by the émigré. Nobody is a collaborator until they collaborate; and there were a great many surprises about who ended up collaborating and who did not after the German occupation of France in 1940.

Partly this is a basic principle of justice, according to which nobody can be condemned, either morally or legally, until they have actually done something. No matter how certain we might be of their future behaviour, there still remains the distinctively human possibility that they will surprise us (for better or for worse). This also applies to the criminological advice given to police forces: no matter how statistically confident we are that a competent adult from a socio-economically deprived part of town will go on to commit a crime, this can never on its own justify "prior restraint". (Only in cases of severe mental illness, where there is a demonstrable risk to other people, can such restraint be justified.) And by the time the person reaches his death bed, his life becomes the sum of his actions, and that is all we have: we will never know what would have happened if he had been forced to act in an unlucky situation. No matter how confident I am that the émigré would have collaborated, or that the inner city child would commit a crime, if he lives his life through to the end without doing it, then all my suspicions have been made meaningless.

Jean-Paul Sartre has an amusing way of making a similar point, in terms of the dying man's regrets that he was "unable" – because of circumstances being against him – to achieve more in his life. Sartre's philosophical writing always has a literary quality to it, so it is worth quoting at length:

> For many have but one resource to sustain them in their misery, and that is to think, "Circumstances have been against me, I was worthy to be something much better than I have been. I admit I have never had a great love or a great friendship; but that is because I never met a man or a woman who were worthy of it; if I have not

written any very good books, it is because I had not the leisure to do so; or, if I have had no children to whom I could devote myself it is because I did not find the man I could have lived with. So there remains within me a wide range of abilities, inclinations and potentialities, unused but perfectly viable, which endow me with a worthiness that could never be inferred from the mere history of my actions." But in reality and for the existentialist, there is no love apart from the deeds of love; no potentiality of love other than that which is manifested in loving; there is no genius other than that which is expressed in works of art. The genius of Proust is the totality of the works of Proust; the genius of Racine is the series of his tragedies, outside of which there is nothing. Why should we attribute to Racine the capacity to write yet another tragedy when that is precisely what he did not write? In life, a man commits himself, draws his own portrait and there is nothing but that portrait. (Sartre [1946] 2005)

Sartre saw the cardinal sin as being the avoidance of responsibility (what he called "bad faith") by shifting the blame onto others or onto circumstances. The dying plaintiff in the quotation asks to be judged against what she could have done in more favourable circumstances. Importantly, however, this cuts both ways: if she is asking for more favourable circumstances to be considered, she should also ask for less favourable circumstances to be considered as well, for life could always have been better or worse. And then the judgement is *wide open*, to the point where judgement becomes impossible. Proust might have written more if circumstances had been better, but he might also have written less, or nothing at all, if any number of infinite possible circumstances had transpired. If we consider one potentiality then in fairness we have to consider them all; and since we cannot possibly consider them all, we should consider none, and simply hold the person responsible for what she decided to do in the situations she found herself in.

The meaningfulness of the regrets Sartre is considering depends on an open future in which to do something about them. On the deathbed it is too late for regrets in this sense. But if my future is open and I can still afford to make plans and begin projects, then expressing regret can be the first stage in facing the future with greater resolve. This is one way to understand the idea of taking responsibility for one's past mistakes. When I say "I regret doing X" or "I am ashamed of having done Y", it actually means "I will henceforth strive to avoid doing X" or "I will try to make up for having done Y". By placing my present self in relation to specific past decisions made in situations, I can thus also place myself in relation to anticipated future situations. The full meaning of the regret can then be revealed by what the agent *does* go on to do in the days and weeks and years following the statement of regret. If the woman regrets not having written very many good books at the age of fifty, the regret will be made meaningful only if she goes on to write a good book.

RESULTANT LUCK

In the previous two sections I attempted to reconcile constitutive luck and situational luck with the possibility of holding people responsible. My strategy has been to shift attention away from the agent's isolated decision and towards his life and identity. Nagel's third and fourth categories of moral luck concern the causes and effects of action. Along with Nagel, I will not be discussing the causes of action, since that essentially concerns the enormously complicated debate about free will and determinism. This section will therefore concern the effects of action, otherwise known as outcome luck or resultant luck. Here are my versions of three examples from Nagel (1979).

The first concerns the *creation of risk*: two drivers, A and A*, drive equally recklessly. This means that, subjectively, they both equally disregard the same known risks and refrain equally from showing due care and attention; objectively, they each drive equally dangerously. Driver A hits and kills a (well-behaved) pedestrian; driver A* gets home safely. Driver A is guilty of manslaughter, and driver A*, if she is caught at all, is guilty of dangerous driving. Driver A suffers a much greater penalty than driver A*, and the difference is entirely due to luck.

The second concerns the *complete attempt*: two assassins, B and B*, are attempting to kill their targets, T and T* respectively. Both assassins have methodically prepared themselves in terms of equipment and situation, both pull the trigger with the full intention of killing their targets. B successfully kills T, but B* is foiled by a bird flying in the path of the bullet, so T* survives. B is caught and sentenced to life in prison for murder; B* is caught and sentenced to ten years in prison for attempted murder. The difference is entirely due to luck. Note that the full description of the act might not be available at the time of performance, or even shortly afterwards. If B *wounds* T on Tuesday, but T does not die from his wounds until Friday, then the Tuesday act does not become murder until Friday. This is not changing the past facts, but the significance of the past facts.[8]

The third concerns *decisions under uncertainty*: two political leaders, C and C*, decide to "appease" nearby dangerous tyrants, H and H* respectively, by accepting each of their "final" demands (the annexation of neighbouring territory). H interprets C's appeasement as weakness, and soon launches a full-scale continental war, involving death and destruction on an unprecedented scale. H* interprets C*'s appeasement as deft and conciliatory, and rewards C* with new trade contracts, and no further aggressive impulses. C is remembered by history as a coward, a dupe or a traitor, who could have stopped H but failed to; C* is remembered as a skilled peacemaker.

In all three cases, concludes Nagel, the moral judgements we or a court are inclined to make do not seem to be immune to luck, and therefore in important respects are unfair on the agents. How do we respond to this? The first thing to notice is that all of Nagel's examples involve explicit comparisons, as when we say that A is less lucky than A*. In each case, Nagel is taking up the view of a scientist performing an experiment to compare the outcome of the test sample against the control sample while holding all extraneous variables constant.

Now recall the "epistemic argument" I adduced in the last section, according to which we cannot ever know if the émigré Frenchman would have collaborated under the Nazi occupation if he had stayed. Counterfactual history is fascinating, but it is not a serious pursuit for professional historians precisely because of the sheer complexities involved. It is important that in all three examples, Nagel stipulates that the two protagonists are the same in all relevant mental properties. But the epistemic argument asks: how can we (the reader, the court, the historian) know this? We can only judge by outward behaviour. Even though we know A and A* are driving equally erratically (or we know they have consumed an equal amount of alcohol), we cannot know whether one of them is actually much more in control of her car than the other, despite appearances (whether she can handle the alcohol better). All we know is that A hits the pedestrian and A* does not; perhaps A was slightly less careful, had slightly slower reflexes, was momentarily distracted – but most of this we cannot know. In addition, Nagel has set up the scenario as essentially comparative, in order to highlight the luck. But normally, what happens is simply what happens. If the driver drives recklessly and hits a pedestrian, then her first thought should be the shock and horror at having hit someone, and her second thought should be about how stupid she was to take such a risk. It would take a special kind of callousness to dwell on how "unlucky" she was.

With regard to the assassination attempts, we first have to distinguish complete and incomplete attempts: an attempt is complete if it is irrevocable. Once the bullet has left the gun, there is nothing either assassin can do to voluntarily prevent the intended action. In contrast, I can choose to interrupt my planned murder in any number of ways before firing the gun. (Whether my plans are advanced enough for me to be charged with a "criminal attempt" is a question, but there is much less of a role for luck.) The point about *in*complete attempts is that the best evidence of the agent's intention is her success. Prior to the pulling of the trigger, the situation was still entirely up to the agent, with no room for luck: it is always possible for her to chicken out at the last moment. On the other hand, Nagel was writing about completed attempts. But notice here the selectivity of his comparison. Normally, if B shoots and kills T, then we assume that this is what she intended to do, and so there is no thought of any luck involved. If she hits T, she will not say "how lucky!" By extension, our first impulse is to hold her responsible for murder – and B herself knows she will be tried for murder, if caught – without reflecting on the many, many things that did *not* happen to prevent her (a piano did not fall on her, a hurricane did not strike, aliens did not invade ...).

Finally, with regard to C appeasing H, the dictator, who goes on to wreak havoc: C will certainly feel bad that he misjudged H, he will certainly regret ignoring the advice not to trust H. He will probably have to resign. But will C think of himself as *unlucky*? After all, C is not responsible for H's decision to wreak havoc. And as with all speculation in history, it is hard to know if C really could have stopped H if the latter was determined enough. The main thing is that here, unlike the other two resultant luck cases, C can reassure himself somewhat that he really did do what he thought was best at the time, and that many others supported his decision as well.

This is not a complete refutation of Nagel, and there has been a lot written in response to his article. As a partial conclusion I will say only that the threat of luck to morality is less than he worries it is, but still somewhat of a threat. It would be tempting to fall back to the Kantian position, according to which the agent's intention is all that is morally relevant in assessing and comparing actions. On the other hand, this is evidently not what we do in all sorts of contexts of evaluation in human life, including the law. We should not attempt to separate action and consequences, for the simple reason that when we act, we *aim* at producing those consequences; we do not aim at producing the act. When I want to call the lift, the final goal of my bodily movements is not the moving of my index finger. This extension of action beyond the body and into the chaotic world will necessarily make me vulnerable to luck.

In the remainder of this chapter I want to move on to Williams's examples from his own "Moral Luck" (1981d) article. Williams agrees that there is a certain threat from luck, but makes some different points about the role it plays in our lives. Above all, while Nagel is mainly interested in the judgements of external observers, Williams is more interested in the protagonists' own judgements of themselves.

WILLIAMS'S LORRY-DRIVER AND GAUGUIN

Unlike Nagel's drivers, Williams's lorry-driver (Williams 1981d: 28) is neither reckless nor negligent. Quite the opposite: he is sober and alert, driving along a familiar road under the speed limit, his brakes have been recently checked, he himself is skilled and experienced. Nevertheless a child runs out from between parked cars, the driver is unable to avoid him, and the child is killed. I have chosen to use the passive voice "is killed" to stress that the driver is in no way culpable or blameworthy, either legally or morally; and yet he was causally responsible for the death. Williams introduces a new term, "agent-regret", to describe the driver's feelings. This is to be distinguished (a) from *regret*, which is merely the wish that things had been otherwise, and which is what one characteristically feels in response to a bad event which one had nothing to do with; and (b) from *remorse*, which is the direct awareness of having been causally and morally responsible for something bad that happened to someone. Agent-regret, then, involves causal but not moral responsibility: I feel bad for what I unwittingly and non-negligently did.

Interestingly, Nagel sees no problem of *moral* luck here, since the driver was not culpable (Nagel 1979: 28). Like many philosophers, Nagel is assuming that the voluntary is essential to morality. And part of the point of Williams's article is to challenge this assumption. What Williams stresses is that the driver cannot detach himself from his having killed the child. The spectators will no doubt try to console the driver by reminding him that it was not his fault, and thereby inviting him to take a more spectatorial (non-causal) perspective on the event – but it is important that he not make this transition to normal regret too quickly, for that would suggest that he has not appreciated the gravity of what he has done.

Even if nobody else can or would blame him, the driver will typically blame himself, and run through all sorts of scenarios in the form of "If only I …". In addition, he will feel a certain obligation to offer apologies and maybe some gesture of rectification towards the child's family, an obligation that would not be undermined by knowledge that the family received a handsome insurance pay-out.

And this regretful self-blame not only makes sense to us, it is also what we would expect of him.[9]

The example of Gauguin is more complicated. For ease of discussion, let me offer the following schematic summary (with invented dates) of the life of the painter Paul Gauguin:

> Gauguin marries, and by 1850 they have three children. Gauguin is increasingly unhappy in his Paris banking job, and has begun to dabble in painting in the evenings. As yet he does not have any evidence of talent, but he enjoys the painting more and more, and is more and more frustrated that his job and his family are preventing him from attending to it properly. Suddenly he abandons job and family, and travels to Tahiti. There he paints and paints for ten years, returning to Paris with his canvases in 1860, and meets wide popular acclaim. During the ten years his family suffer greatly, as Gauguin knew they would – Mrs Gauguin's own family was already poor, and there is of course no welfare state.[10]

Williams asks: how are we to judge Gauguin? What are we to hold him morally responsible for? The simple answer would be to say that the end justified the means and therefore that, while it is sad that his family had to suffer and that he neglected his freely assumed familial duties to them, if the result was such great art then it must have been worth it. However, at the time of abandoning his family, Gauguin had *no idea* of his future success. Even in purely risk–benefit terms, the probability that he had the talent and that he would be able to bring it to fruition on Tahiti were vanishingly small, not to mention all the myriad logistical hurdles in getting the finished artworks to the Paris dealers intact. When we compare the low probability of success with the near certainty that his family would suffer greatly without his income, then abandoning them for this frivolous venture would seem deserving of the severest of condemnation. Importantly, if the venture does go badly, then there would be no way that he could sincerely reassure himself – and others – that he did what he thought was best at the time.

Williams then introduces the notion of "retrospective justification" (1981d: 24). When we spoke of justification in Chapter 1, we
were discussing a temporally absolute concept. Given the circumstances at the time, either I was or I was not justified in breaking
the law (e.g. in self-defence). In contrast, Williams suggests that
there is a change in the justification status. In 1850, the abandonment was not justified. But Gauguin's hugely fortuitous success in
1860 retrospectively altered the metaphysical status of the original
abandonment, from not justified to justified. The problem of moral
luck, for Williams, is then the following. Between 1850 and 1860,
Gauguin was the beneficiary of a massive amount of luck, and this
changed what we are inclined to say about him, morally. But this
means that in 1850, or *at any time*, we would not be in a position
to condemn an act as morally unjustified because it may yet turn
out to be justified by subsequent events. But this also means that
we cannot speak of the abandonment as justified even after Gauguin's successful return in 1860 – for *further* events might yet go
on to un-justify it!

Note that Williams does not mean *moral* justification, where the
moral benefits of success can be measured against its moral costs
and risks. Perhaps if Gauguin had been a doctor, then emigration
to Tahiti to work with the poor might morally justify abandoning the family to their bleak fate (although *Mrs* Gauguin might not
agree, on which, see below). Instead, Williams just means justification *simpliciter*, such that immorality might sometimes be justified. This might be plausible in the case of Gauguin's great artistic
achievement, but Williams has a more controversial claim in mind.
One of Williams's enduring themes in his work is his criticism of
moralism, the belief that moral considerations ought to trump all
others. Not only can great art outweigh morality as in (supposedly)
Gauguin's case, but, more controversially, an individual's personal
"project" can also outweigh it *for that individual*, regardless of the
public or commercial value of that project. For Williams, "project"
is a semi-technical term, and denotes those commitments, relationships and memberships that give meaning to an individual's
life, that give her reason to get out of bed in the morning, that
support her life enough to *then* be able to take morality seriously,
in so far as she does. If the promotion of an individual's project

requires an immoral act from that individual, then we should not be surprised if the individual chooses to act immorally. (Note that Williams's view still allows a saint to make morality her "project".)

Because of the importance of the project to Gauguin's life, if a third party were to *blame* Gauguin for abandoning his family – abandoning a woman he freely chose to marry, and abandoning children he freely chose to beget, after all – there is a real risk of the blame not finding purchase. This need not be because Gauguin was a self-absorbed artist; he may well have been morally serious, and the abandonment might have caused him genuine pain, but he felt he simply had to leave. Certainly he wasn't taking the easy way out in order to avoid his family duties, since the venture had plenty of risks of its own.

Williams then makes an important distinction (*ibid.*: 25, 36) between the two different kinds of regret that might arise from two different kinds of project failure. If Gauguin had suffered an "extrinsic" failure in the form of an obstacle to the project, such as breaking his leg, or losing the canvases at sea, he would be sad but he might still have felt that it was worth having a go. However, if Gauguin had suffered the particular "intrinsic" failure of discovering that he definitely had no talent (i.e. that there was no more point in trying or hoping), then the abandonment would at that point become permanently *un*justified, and he could experience bitter regret for wronging his family for nothing. At one level, of course, he is responsible for the family's suffering, but he is prepared to accept that while the promise of artistic success beckoned. Once such success is definitely ruled out, then all he has left is the deeper responsibility for the harm he has caused.

Ultimately, Williams's discussion, while insightful about the place and role that moral responsibility for a particular wrong can have in someone's life, is too simplistic in its account of justification. In the end Williams seems to give too much weight to *Gauguin's* perspective on what counts as justified. It is likely that Gauguin believed, in 1850, that artistic success would justify the abandonment, and then believed, in 1860, that success had justified it. If he hadn't, he would have returned home, after all. But just because Gauguin thinks it justified does not mean that he is immune to moral blindness, or that anybody else ought to accept that it was justified. It is unlikely, for example, that Mrs Gauguin would have thought the project justified, even after her husband's artistic success. Why should his version of events count more than hers, especially when they were in a joint enterprise together up until the abandonment? There is a slim chance that Mrs Gauguin would have felt the unwilling sacrifice of herself and her children to have been a price worth paying for her husband's artistic success, but she would not be behaving unreasonably or ungratefully if she refused to ever see him again. Finally, the full meaning of the abandonment itself depended on what happened to the wife and children. If one of the children had died of starvation, for example, or if Mrs Gauguin had committed suicide, then Gauguin's justification attempt becomes less plausible and verges on the indecent.

Williams even goes so far as to suggest that we, the art-loving public, should be "glad" that he abandoned his family (*ibid.*: 37). But as Raimond Gaita has forcefully argued (2004: 240), Williams is assuming that the abandonment was necessary for the creation of the artworks. Gauguin probably thought so, but why should we accept his self-serving verdict? As we saw in our discussion of the epistemic argument in response to Nagel, speculating about counterfactuals is a fool's errand. Was there really no possibility for Gauguin to paint in Paris while staying with his family? In the end, all we can do, says Gaita, is to be glad about the painting, condemn the abandonment, but accept that he had strong reasons for abandoning them – and leave out all talk of justification.

6

ROLE-RESPONSIBILITY

The first half of this book was about retrospective responsibility, with the focus question of what it means to hold an agent responsible now for a discrete act in the past. In this second Part, I want to examine prospective responsibility. Instead of being held responsible for having done something, I am taking responsibility for something yet to come. A certain kind of prospective responsibility is already implied by the retrospective structure. Having been held responsible in the present for my past acts, I now know that I may be held responsible in the future for my present acts – perhaps this means that I will be a bit more careful, I might think things through a bit more, I might look for more reasons or evidence to support the act I am contemplating, and so on. One reason we praise a person by calling her "responsible" – that is, as a character trait – is if she is reliably disposed to consider the future with greater care, imagination and sensitivity than an average person.

In this chapter I want to examine a particular kind of prospective responsibility, that associated with the occupation of a role. So while the class of people under consideration in Part I was essentially any adult human being, and indeed many older children, in this Part we are distinguishing the responsibility of those occupying the role from those who do not. Some roles are in principle open to anybody, but other roles are less accessible.

But there is an ambiguity right away. Sometimes a role is defined (e.g. a job description) in terms of its "responsibilities", but this word is often little more than a synonym for "duty", as in: "It is the nurse's responsibility to check the blood pressure at regular intervals", or "The manager is responsible for getting a certain project done on time and under budget". The latter is a bit more complicated, since there are many more contingencies that may require flexibility and attention by the manager, and this will be relevant in what follows. In contrast to both, however, what I have centrally in mind is being responsible *for* and *to another person* in virtue of the role I occupy. As a doctor, I am responsible for my patients and to my patients; as a teacher I am responsible for and to my students; as a parent I am responsible for and to my children.

The two prepositions "for" and "to" are important. In being responsible *for* another, I have to, again following the etymology, *respond* to them: that is, to look after them in the manner required by the role, to attend to their needs and welfare, and to ensure that I am continually up to the role. This requires flexibility and attention, as with the manager. But if one is to perform the role well, it also takes an empathetic concern over the short and long term, a deep-seated interest in the other's well-being, and an emotional investment in their life. It will involve not just attention but the cultivation of a distinctive kind of attentiveness, a certain readiness to act, and an active resistance to the forces of boredom, irritation and insecurity that occasionally accompany any role.

Being responsible *to* can have different objects at the same time. If the role is institutional (a hospital doctor and a schoolteacher), then I will be responsible to my superiors for the purposes of hierarchical management. If the role is professional, I will be responsible to my professional body and, more abstractly, to the ideals that define my profession. But in any role I will be responsible *to the beneficiaries*: the patients, the students, my children, and so on. Being responsible to the beneficiary means acknowledging their claim upon you in virtue of your role-defined relationship, acknowledging their right to your expertise, your attention and your care, acknowledging their right to criticize you. In the case of role-defined relationships between adults and children, there is a further ambiguity about the word "to". The young pupil is responsible to the teacher in the sense of owing obedience. And yet the teacher is responsible to the pupil in the sense of owing her an education; and part of this role-responsibility will involve acknowledging the child's *future* right, once she achieves an age to benefit from the fruits of her earlier education, to criticize the teacher for having failed her.

It is worth stressing that prospective responsibility can become retrospective: if a doctor fails in her duty of care to a patient, then she can be held responsible by that patient (through a lawsuit accusing the doctor of negligence), by her profession, or by the criminal law – that is, she can be held responsible for failing to respond appropriately.

THE DOCTOR

I want to look at the role of the doctor in this section, but most of what I say can be said about any of the "caring" professions – nurse, social worker, priest, teacher – and to a certain degree about any other professions who have clients (lawyers, engineers, accountants). A lot will be relevant to any employee working in the public service as well. I do not have the space to consider all these roles, however.

The doctor's role seems to be relatively clear. On the one hand, there is her role in promoting and restoring her patient's health and alleviating his suffering as much as possible. There are certain philosophical and medical debates about the precise meaning of health, but for our purposes it is enough to understand it intuitively as the normal physiological function and comfort instrumentally required to allow the patient to lead a minimally decent life that involves some meaningful project. On the other hand, the doctor's role is defined explicitly by the medical profession. The profession admits people to medical school according to certain criteria, the profession assesses them, reassesses them, and licenses them, and the profession is responsible for most of the discipline of its members, and for co-operating with the legal system in serious cases. Medical training takes a long time, and this can be justified by the sheer quantity of explicit and implicit information, rules, procedures and skills that have to be learned, practised and tested, but also by the length of time needed to *become* a doctor, that is, to see, think and act spontaneously as a doctor, to develop reliable clinical judgement, to orient oneself in the medical world, to assume the authority to run a medical team, often under high-pressure situations when so much is at stake.

A doctor is retrospectively responsible for her free, informed, intentional and reckless acts and their reasonably foreseeable proximate consequences, just as any ordinary person would be. She can also be held responsible for negligence, both in a general sense and especially a role-related sense; because she has this greater role-related responsibility, more can be reasonably expected from her, and she is therefore at greater risk of negligence than non-doctors. If a surgeon cuts a patient open and accidentally severs a major artery resulting in the patient's bleeding to death, then the surgeon will probably have been negligent; this means that it should have occurred to her that there might be a major artery near the cutting site, she should have checked its exact route through the site before cutting, she should have taken appropriate care while cutting to avoid the likely eventuality that the artery would be severed (given that she knew its route), and she should have put in place procedures to deal with the severed artery (given the likelihood of severing it despite her due care).

So far this is not much more than we saw in Part I. But there is sometimes more to role-related responsibility than fulfilling minimal legitimate expectations from professional peers and healthcare managers and patients, and more than avoiding negligence lawsuits, and this is where it becomes interesting. There is an additional, unenforceable layer of responsibility which some doctors accept to different degrees, and at different stages in their careers; this has to do with the different *personal* meanings and ideals that the word "doctor" has.

Consider the attitude to being on and off duty. Some doctors see themselves as ordinary employees. They were hired on the basis of their knowledge and skills, they sign a contract stipulating work duties and hours in exchange for a salary, they go to work during those hours and they fulfil those duties satisfactorily using their knowledge and skills. But at the end of their shift they have had enough, they hang up their white coat and they go home to watch the footie. They see themselves as having a right to "me-time", especially when they suffer from the understandable compassion fatigue after a long day in the presence of so much suffering and despair that remains untreatable despite their knowledge and skills. I want to stress right away that I have nothing against this kind of "duteous" doctor, and in fact I greatly admire them for choosing and sticking with such a difficult job. Different doctors will be more or less duteous at different stages of their career, or in different aspects of their job. And there is a real question about whether one can cultivate any sort of serious project outside medicine (including a rich family life) without becoming more "duteous" at work.

Other doctors see themselves as *taking* a greater responsibility, a responsibility associated more with their role in society rather than their role in the institution, and as such their responsibility continues after the end of their shift. They see themselves as more responsible to the ideals of the profession and to their patients. Once this sort of "responsive" doctor (as I shall call her) accepts a patient into her care, he is *her* patient, and his illness and suffering is *her* business, where the "her" refers to something much more than the institutional allocation procedures. The responsive doctor cares about her patient as a person rather than as a locus of physiological defects; she is able to avoid getting worn down by the institutional politics and the sheer drudgery of so much medical work. Even when off duty, this doctor will remain concerned for her patient. Indeed, she will also be more sensitive to the needs of people who are not formally allocated to her as patients, that is, to neighbours, to relatives, to fellow plane travellers, and to all manner of people she meets in the shopping mall or in the pub or at the football match.

The responsive doctor's actual behaviour, observed by a third party, might in many details be no different than that of the duteous doctor. The difference lies in the *spirit* with which the two doctors go about their duties. I take this notion of "spirit" from Iris Murdoch, and her famous example of M and D (1970: 17). M is an older woman, with a grown-up son, and that son has married D, much to M's disapproval. However, M has a strong sense of social norms, and she makes sure that her behaviour towards D is impeccable. Behind that behaviour, M could continue nurturing her disapproval indefinitely. "However," Murdoch continues:

> the M of the example is an intelligent and well-intentioned person, capable of self-criticism, capable of giving careful and just attention to an object which confronts her. M tells herself: "I am old-fashioned and conventional. I may be prejudiced and narrow-minded. I may be snobbish. I am certainly jealous. Let me look again." ... D is discovered to be not vulgar but refreshingly simple, not undignified but spontaneous, not noisy but gay, not tiresomely juvenile but delightfully youthful, and so on. And as I say, *ex hypothesi*, M's outward behaviour, beautiful from the start, in no way alters. (*Ibid.*)

Importantly, the responsive doctor can adopt Murdoch's "careful and just attention" in dealing with the patient's fear, loneliness and humiliation and existential anxieties, especially in the presence of death, while the duteous doctor is more likely to call the nurse, the social worker or the chaplain and let them deal with the patient in accordance with *their* expertise. The responsive doctor is more likely to interpret her patient's whingeing, self-absorption and hypochondria as natural responses to this unfamiliar and often unfriendly hospital setting. Whatever the reality of today's doctors, I think it remains the case that most patients see their doctors as having a priestly quality, a moral authority and a humane wisdom, and it is the responsive doctor who responds to this expectation as well.[1]

What is most interesting about the responsive doctor is the *reason* she gives for taking on this additional responsibility, the reason for staying on beyond her shift to hold the hand of the distressed patient in bed 17. She says simply, "It's because I'm a doctor". She knows that you know that she is a doctor in the professional-institutional sense, of course. So in giving that as her reason, and in not giving any further reasons, she is expecting you to take her meaning in a richer, more abstract sense, a sense that she assumes you already understand. Again, there are plenty of intelligible reasons to become a doctor, and this is the stuff of conversations between parents and high school students throughout the world. And it may be that the responsive doctor started her career with those reasons in mind, before later losing them. I am alluding here to my point in the section "Constitutive luck" in Chapter 5 about identifying with one's job to such a degree and for enough time that it becomes an essential part of one's existence, such that one can no longer conceive of oneself as having had a choice. In so far as the responsive doctor is unable to give further reasons for doing so much more than the duteous doctor, she is almost describing herself as lacking choice.

The idea of lacking choice always rings alarm bells. At worst, it implies the loss of autonomy and independence. At best, it implies in this case an identification with the role to such an extent that one merely fulfils the expectations of others served by the role, and thereby hides behind or dissolves into the role – this was epitomized by Jean-Paul Sartre's example of the waiter (Sartre 1993: 167). However, lacking choice need not be such a threat to autonomy. If we define autonomy, very roughly, as the capacity to act on one's deepest desires, then yes, autonomy can be inhibited by hiding behind a role. But adopting a role can also clarify one's deepest desires, and thereby *enhance* one's autonomy. Many people are not sure what they want, and are driven by momentary whims; they then find their role, and this releases them to be and do what they most deeply want to be and do.

The notion of a *calling* or *vocation* is something that one obeys without awareness of any choice in the matter. It is even incorrect to describe the responsive doctor, as I did earlier, as "taking" a greater responsibility; instead she is merely acknowledging that she *has* a greater responsibility. In fact, I would even suggest she does not experience her responsibility as "greater", for she is not comparing herself to her colleagues; she simply discovers what *she* must do.[2]

The responsive doctor's sense of a calling is something deeply personal, but without being merely personal. An example of the merely personal is one's taste in music or clothing, where nothing of real importance depends on this. The doctor's response is personal not only in the sense that she has a different response from her colleagues, but mainly in the sense that her response partly constitutes her identity. And yet her experience of her role is of something very much *im*personal and objective: her attention is very much focused on the patient, and on the objective standards of medical care. There is an apparent paradox here, in that the doctor may discover a good deal about herself only by thinking about the world outside herself. And however distant she might feel on occasion from her colleagues or from her family and friends, she still understands herself as part of a community of medicine and indeed of a community of humankind, and she is still in principle accessible to arguments and reasons about, say, the best way to treat a particular disease – she is not an arrogant isolationist, or shut off in her own private sect.

The responsive doctor may respond to a calling by the profession as a whole, or to some sub-discipline of the profession (paediatrics, surgery, etc.), or to some extension of the profession such as working in a war zone or in the third world. In the latter case, the first-world doctor may declare that she cannot "in all conscience" avoid her responsibility to patients in the third world "where the need is so much greater". In this latter case we can see how far away this concept of responsibility is from the retrospective responsibility of Part I, which was so often linked to blameworthiness. The third-world doctor's understanding of her responsibility is personal in the sense of "supererogatory", that is, it is intelligibly admirable, but those doctors who do not experience such a calling are not thereby blameworthy in any sense.

THE PARENT

While the object of the parent's responsibility – the child – might be more specific and longer-term than that of the doctor's responsibility, all other aspects of the role are much more poorly defined. There is no training course to become a parent, no licensing procedure, no clear professional disciplinary procedure; there is no clear distinction between on and off duty, there is no employment contract and job description with a particular institution, there are no holidays and no explicit provisions for days off work due to illness. And there is very little money or social prestige! In one sense it is very familiar, since we all remember our own parents or guardians, and because many of the tasks involved are fairly simple. But in another sense there is definitely a core of the experience that is hard for a parent to communicate to a non-parent, no matter how many parenting manuals the latter has read. In the previous section, as elsewhere in the book, I have been exploring the idea that some kinds of responsibility depend on a deep response to an objective claim by another. This idea is much more plausible in parenting. The full meaning of parental responsibility, I suggest, is most keenly grasped during the first few days and weeks after the excitement and anxiety of the birth. I want to discuss three kinds of realization, each of which can indeed be quite frightening.

First is the realization – especially acute at three in the morning – of just how vulnerable the baby is, how utterly needy, and yet how inarticulate about her needs; a realization about just how easily the rest of her life could be damaged and undermined by adult clumsiness or by brute bad luck; a realization of just how wrong such damage would be, given the purity of the child's radiant innocence; and a realization that *I and my partner* are the ones who mainly have to meet these needs, and protect her from all the evils of the world. (And for single parents, this stark realization is not even tempered by the awareness of the other partner's presence, assistance and good will.)

At one point the baby cries and cries and cries, and nothing seems to work. You try holding her, rocking her, singing to her; you offer her a breast, a bottle, a dummy, she does not want any of it; you plonk her in the baby carriage and go for a long, long walk; you take her to doctors and nurses and get fobbed off with some vague story about "colic". And still she cries. This is the purest source of parenting responsibility. There is no decision to be made here, and only minimal concrete duties; and by this stage any feelings of love and awe and pride have dwindled. All that is left is the brute claim and the brute response – and a lot of it so frustratingly fruitless. And when the little bastard *finally* falls asleep at three in the morning, you collapse not only from physical exhaustion but also from the knowledge that it may well all begin again in a few hours. And your last thought before snatching slumber is: "This is it, this is what being a parent's all about."

143

The second kind of realization is of how the baby's dependency and your loving responsibility now combine to make *you* more vulnerable than you have ever been in your adult life. It is hard to describe this vulnerability except by comparing it to the sort of misfortunes that non-parents can imagine befalling them. One can vaguely imagine the house burning down, having one's legs amputated following a car crash, getting cancer, perhaps being tortured; and one can vaguely imagine dealing with these misfortunes more or less stoically. But imagining one's child being injured or traumatized or killed is a kind of pain of a wholly different dimension. Or imagining that the child is suffering and that you are not there to help her. Or worst of all, imagining that the child is injured or killed through a moment's inattention or clumsiness on your part. I suggest that these hypothetical imaginings express particularly painfully what parental responsibility means, even before anything bad has even happened to the child.

Finally, the third kind of realization is of the pervasiveness, relentlessness and endlessness of it all. Even with the help of grandmothers and nannies, caring for a well-behaved and developmentally normal small child is hard graft, with complicated logistics, and often tediously dull. And on bad days it is best not to think about the fact that the responsibility never ends, although the child will obviously change in various ways. Any other project that was so time and soul-consuming would at least allow the consoling thoughts of "If worse comes to worst I can just walk away" or "I'll just do another month and then see". But the nature of parental responsibility is such as to forbid such a thought, even in jest. Of course it does happen that parents collapse and the child has to be raised by a relative or given up for adoption. But that collapse is not preceded by the attentive weighing of pros and cons until a determinate threshold is reached, it is the result of crushing despair and a loss of effective agency. The main reason it is so hard to walk away from your child is precisely because she remains *your* child even after you have walked away, and this explains at the very least the ambivalence of most biological mothers at the thought of how their child might be faring in their adoptive family.

For some couples, these three kinds of realization come as a massive shock. Sometimes this shock brings out the best in a relationship, sometimes the worst; sometimes it ruptures it altogether, and one of the parents legs it. But the shock also brings home just how ill informed their previous expressed desire for a child turned out to be. Indeed, in law, if "consent" is too ill informed it is no longer consent, as when a homeowner is persuaded to sell their house for a thousand pounds.

Unconditional parental responsibility

Parental responsibility is *unconditional*; this means that the responsibility exists regardless of what the child is, or does, or becomes. Sometimes this notion is described as unconditional *love*, but this can be misleading because of the widespread assumption that love has to do primarily with a spontaneous feeling, and what is more, with a feeling that the subject experiences purely passively and randomly. It is perfectly natural for a parent not to experience loving feelings on certain occasions, but for this not to undermine the responsibility or the sense of responsibility. Indeed, it is perfectly compatible to lack loving feelings towards my noisy, smelly, vulgar teenage son while still having a robust sense of unconditional responsibility towards him.

Sometimes the notion is also described as unconditional *duty*, but I suggest this term is also inadequate. A duty is an entity that comes between the performer and the beneficiary; the performer has the duty in mind, without necessarily having any interest in the beneficiary, or in whether the beneficiary actually benefited from the dutiful act. Duties can be humiliating to perform, can be performed smugly, or grudgingly, and are perfectly compatible with resenting or hating the beneficiary on whom they have been imposed. We saw something of this distinction in the two kinds of doctors: roughly, the duteous doctor is more interested in doing his duty, while the responsive doctor is more interested in the patients. Similarly, one can fulfil all one's parental duties and yet fail as a parent. In contrast, unconditional responsibility keeps the beneficiary, and the beneficiary's needs, welfare and interests, at the forefront of one's consciousness. When the parent is woken up at three in the morning by his infant daughter's screams, he does not pause to reflect on what his duty is in such a situation; rather, he responds to her directly. In getting up, he is not aware of any duty that he is fulfilling in the process; he is motivated directly by his daughter.[3]

There are three aspects to the parent's unconditional responsibility. The first is this permanent state of "on call", this readiness to attend to your child at any hour of the day or night, unlike the duteous doctors and teachers. Before that, the second aspect involves the willingness to take unconditional responsibility for whatever comes out of the womb, regardless of its appearance or handicaps, regardless of the parents' involuntary hopes and expectations before the birth, and regardless of the parents' own spontaneous positive or negative feelings after the birth. Often, perhaps after most births, the parents find it easy to love their child, and the sense of unconditional responsibility follows naturally. Sometimes they might find it very difficult to love the child, and to cultivate an unconditional responsibility for her. More generally, there are deep paradoxes in our attitudes to the handicapped, and especially to the visibly handicapped. In many ways, Western society has made great progress in catering to the needs of the handicapped, although there is certainly more that can be done. Certainly, most able-bodied people do not find any difficulty nowadays in interacting without condescension with fellow students, peers or colleagues who are handicapped. So this broad acceptance is one side of the paradox; the other side is the widespread belief that certain handicaps can unproblematically justify abortion, and that the birth of a handicapped child is a great tragedy for a family.

The third aspect of unconditional responsibility is the readiness to "be there" for the child, whatever it takes, for the rest of her life, regardless of what the child does or becomes (I am taking this idea from MacIntyre 1999: 99). This has to be carefully distinguished from smothering the child, especially as she achieves independence in running her own life, living in her own place, making her own money, and managing her own relationships. "Being there" is certainly compatible with leaving your child well alone, and with getting on with one's own projects and interests in a place far away. This attitude is also compatible with the child denying that she needs the parent or owes the parent anything, and with the child and parent not particularly liking each other or having much to say to each other.

"Being there" for the child regardless of what he turns into sometimes generates uncomfortable dilemmas, as when one's teenage child commits a crime and asks you to hide him from the police. Sometimes this dilemma is phrased as a conflict between duty and love, and certainly it would be understandable if the parent ignored his moral or civic duty. However, if the child really did commit the crime, if the police have the moral authority to pursue him and the courts to punish him fairly (we are not talking about a political crime under a dictatorship, for example), then a sense of unconditional responsibility and love towards the child could require that he be handed over to police *for his own good*. In saying this, I am drawing on Jean Hampton's conception of punishment as a form of education which some citizens might need. A real dilemma would be if the parents knew that the police were corrupt, and were looking for a scapegoat; or if the parents felt that prison would brutalize their child in a way that would undo any pedagogical value of the punishment.

At the beginning of this book I quoted from Saint-Exupéry's novel *Le Petit Prince*.[4] In chapter 21 the fox advises the Prince, with reference to his rose, that "You become forever responsible for those whom you tame (*apprivoiser*)." The word "tame" has a clear reference to animals, of course. But there is a larger meaning to the French word. It can also mean "embrace" or "get to know" or even "invest". In embracing, investing in, and getting to know his rose, he takes responsibility for it. Its etymology goes back to the Latin word for "private", as when one brings an animal into one's private domestic space and into one's life. As such, taming is not merely training and reconditioning the animal at arm's length, as it were. It means bringing the animal into one's sphere of care and concern. In doing so, one changes the animal, so that its new identity is forever altered. In that way one is responsible for it forever.

One last thought about unconditional parental responsibility: that is how deeply it can run, in some cases far deeper than rational thought. In his article "On the Necessity of Ideals", Harry Frankfurt (1999) discusses a fascinating example of a woman who decides during her pregnancy that she will surrender the child for adoption after birth. She has plenty of "good reasons" for deciding thus: she is too young, too ambitious, too far away from her family, too lacking in maternal instincts or longings, whatever — and she concludes that it would simply not be fair on the child to keep it. At the same time, she is reassured by the thought of bringing joy to an infertile couple, and she genuinely believes that the child will be better off with an adoptive family. The day comes, the birth is straightforward, the child is born, but when the social worker comes to collect the child, the woman finds she "cannot" give the child up. Frankfurt calls this an example of the necessity of love. Importantly for Frankfurt, the woman has *not* changed her mind, for she still accepts the cogency of the reasons for her earlier decision. But she cannot bring herself to "abandon" (her word) the child. She can offer no reason to the waiting social worker for keeping the child, except to say "It's my child".

This is not at all to suggest that the woman has done the "right" thing, or that love "conquers all". But what she has done can be reliably recognized as an expression of love, and an acceptance of unconditional responsibility despite the lack of reasons that she can offer in her defence. Importantly, of course, the social worker would have to respect the woman's new position on the matter, even if the social worker herself agreed that the child would be better off with adoptive parents for precisely the reasons that the woman originally gave.

PARENTING LICENCES?

Most roles and role-responsibility can be defined with reference to formal norms and standards. Many roles, such as the professions, have a governing body that can admit, discipline and expel members in accordance with how well they fulfil the role-responsibility. Parenting is a glaring exception on both accounts, and it will be instructive to examine one philosopher's notorious proposal to *license* parents. Hugh LaFollette's proposal is all the more interesting because the original 1980 paper generated a great many comments and criticisms, and he tried to respond to many of these by revising his paper in 2010.

At the heart of LaFollette's papers are three simple analogies: with driving licences, with medical licences and with adoption screening – I'll discuss the adoption analogy in moment. Both drivers and doctors have to take a course, and then take a test on their knowledge and skills (indeed, the doctor is continually tested over the course of her career). If successful, they are awarded a licence. The justification for both licensing systems is obvious: whether they have control of a car or a scalpel, these classes of people have an increased capacity to harm other people, and therefore they both have to take greater responsibility when driving or treating.

LaFollette is understandably distressed by the sheer amount of revealed child abuse that goes on in the United States (not to mention his concern about the unrevealed abuse). The current system of monitoring, support and intervention by social workers is, he believes, inadequate because it has to wait for the damage to be done. He sees abused children as the innocent victims of irresponsible people who often lack the knowledge or skills necessary to be minimally good parents. He therefore suggests that aspiring couples be required to take a course, then take a test, in order to gain a parenting licence, which would allow them to keep any child they subsequently produce.[5]

LaFollette is more interested in the principle than in the detail of these tests: presumably once legislators could agree on the principle, then the detail could be worked out by the social workers, psychologists and paediatricians. Of course, the test could not be too difficult; the aim would not be to significantly reduce the number of children born nor to overly increase the burden on foster and adoption care. But then again, the driving test is easy enough for the vast majority of applicants to pass, if necessary on repeated attempts. And while the driving test is obviously not perfect enough to prevent all accidents, at least the state can declare that every person who passes the test has a basic minimum of knowledge and skill to be allowed to drive a harmful vehicle, and that there would be far more accidents without the licensing system. The fact that the medical or the driving test is imperfect is not seen as grounds to abolish it altogether, merely as the starting point for further discussion among policy experts in fine-tuning it from year to year.

Parenting is, of course, far more complex than driving a car, but the test could be based on the fundamental points of agreement among the many parenting manuals, some basic facts of nutrition, the principles and practice of first aid, the milestones of average child development, how the benefits, healthcare and education systems work, and so on. Most couples, with enough effort and preparation, could pass, and so it could also be understood as a test of motivation. Already there exist plenty of voluntary courses, both ante-natal and post-natal, and their content is hardly challenging or controversial. Perhaps a psychological assessment could be part of the test; this might sound draconian to some, says LaFollette, but is it really so outlandish to suggest that someone with a history of violent alcoholism could not become a minimally good parent? In the same way that nobody can claim that they *need* to drive or have a *right* to become a doctor, so too nobody should think of themselves as needing children or having a right to them without regard to the risks to the child.[6]

LaFollette then explains that two *de facto* forms of parenting licence already exist in most countries. First, any couple who want children can apply to adopt one. The couple are thoroughly screened in order to determine whether the parents are suitable, and if so to determine the best fit with available children. The adoption process is deliberately designed to be bi-directional; that is, it is not top-down evaluation and discrimination by social workers; it also involves explaining to the applicant what precisely is involved in raising a child: this helps the applicants to prepare but also to think twice about whether they really want to take on the responsibility. The principle of screening applicants for adoption of non-biologically related children is hardly controversial (although some of the details might be), says LaFollette, so why should the screening of applicants for their biological offspring be?

The second precedent is admittedly very rare. If a woman has shown herself to be repeatedly and predictably incapable of looking after a child in the past, either because of severe mental handicap or because of severe drug addiction or abusive tendencies, then social workers can make a decision to remove the next child at birth, that is, without giving her another chance. This comes close to the concept of "prior restraint": when an individual is considered

so dangerous – usually because of relevant mental health problems – that he can be isolated in a psychiatric institution *before* he
breaks any laws or harms anybody. Prior restraint is difficult to justify legally; it is a lot easier to let the suspect commit the crime and
then pounce on him red-handed. Nevertheless, LaFollette would
argue that the sheer vulnerability and innocence of the child are
such as to justify the significant expansion of this prior restraint
approach, by means of denying failed licence applicants the right
to keep their children.

Response to LaFollette

The fascinating thing about LaFollette's two articles, however, is
their abject failure. As far as I know, there is no serious political
movement, at least not in the Western world, calling for parents
to be licensed. Apart from adoption screening and prior restraint
(which still involves a very small minority of children), there is
nothing close to a parenting licence, and nothing close to the suggestion that existing ante-natal classes be compulsory. So what has
LaFollette been missing? LaFollette's failure reveals something very
interesting about the place of children in families in our society.
LaFollette's own explanation for his failure has to do with a widespread mistaken conception of children as the *property* of their
parents: the liberal state has no business interfering with a citizen's
property unless it is harming someone outside his family. Instead,
says LaFollette, the parent should not be seen as the owner but
rather the trustee, acting in the best interests of the future individual the child will become, and this would justify greater intru-
siveness by the state. LaFollette's explanation for his failure cannot
be the full story, however. There are plenty of people who acknowledge that their children are not property, and who would accept
that they do have a responsibility to tend their interests and needs
– and yet they would still reject the licensing proposal.

Many of LaFollette's critics talk about the practical problems
of designing and implementing the licensing regime, but I accept
LaFollette's point that there is a philosophical matter of principle
that can be discussed here. However, even in the matter of principle,

LaFollette underestimates three things: first, the difficulty of predicting the performance of future parents; second, the sheer plurality of healthy parenting practices; third, the degree to which people identify with their children and which makes them especially sensitive to such an intervention. Let me take these in turn.

The point about prediction is well argued by Lawrence Frisch (1982: 176–7). Strictly speaking, the licensing of car drivers is a matter of testing present competence, rather than an effort to predict future behaviour. But even if we could confidently predict future car-driving behaviour, it is not plausible to try to predict future parenting behaviour, given its complexity, its changeability through time (see next point), but above all the transformative power of parenting. Nobody is transformed by becoming a driver. But precisely because parenting involves such a radical transformation of the person's identity, it is hard to predict how individuals will rise, or fail to rise, to the challenge. It is certainly possible, and is material for a dozen sentimental films, for someone with the worst character traits to suddenly clean his act up when confronted with the claims from the newborn baby.

Second, the point about plurality is not a point that "anything goes", and therefore intervention is always inappropriate. The pluralist can acknowledge that there is better and worse parenting, and that abuse can be defined relatively unambiguously; he can accept the role of the state in monitoring, supporting and eventually intervening. But licensing is much too clumsy a tool to use on prospective parents, because parenting is so much more complicated than driving or medicine, and because good parenting comes in so many more types than good driving or medicine. For a start, a particular couple will require different skills as their child ages and changes; and different couples will require different skills for their different children. So much of parenting involves getting to know one's particular child well, learning how to deal with him – and then getting to know him again and learn how to deal with him again, and again. Not only are couples each very different from one another; not only are children each very different from one another; but the relationships between the two parents and between the particular couple and particular children are very different from one another. Anybody who works with a lot of children on a daily basis, and who interacts occasionally with their parents, will understand this.

A more appropriate approach to this complexity is to realize that some parents abuse their children out of frustration, stress and unhappiness in their own lives. The answer, therefore, is to offer more ongoing state support at every level of the child's development, to improve pre-schools and schools, and to offer longer parental leave. As in so many areas of social welfare, it is the Scandinavian countries who are most advanced in this.

The third response to LaFollette involves understanding more about the precise relationship between parents and children. LaFollette is right to criticize the assumption that children are the property of their parents, but he is mistaken in thinking that they do not *belong* to their parents in a non-proprietary manner, a manner corresponding to the parent's identification with the child.When the parent says, in any number of natural contexts, "She's my child", this is not the same as "It's my pen". At the very least, the parent knows that her child has needs, interests, wishes and a future in a way radically unlike any of the parent's possessions. The parent's capacity to be proud or ashamed of her child presupposes some degree of identification. And this is what makes intervention by social workers, even in clear abuse cases, so harrowing for both child and parent. It is not as if the child and the parent are two physically and metaphysically separate atoms whose separation can be justified by the failure of one to fulfil her quasi-contractual obligations to the other; the separation will directly harm both the parent as an individual and the child as an individual. LaFollette would accept that this is a price worth paying to avoid the far greater harm of abuse. Once again I am pessimistic that the sheer intimacy of the identification relationship can be adequately assessed in cases that do not relate to clear evidence of abuse.

7

RESPONSIBILITY FOR STRANGERS

In the previous chapter I discussed an individual's prospective responsibility for and to another individual, grounded in the relevant formal role (e.g. doctor, parent) that defined their relationship. In this chapter I want to examine the responsibility one might have for a stranger. By "stranger" I mean someone to whom I have no formal duties, other than the general liberal duty to refrain from harming or hindering him without justification. Now, of course, when a patient visits a GP in her surgery for the first time, he is a stranger to her. But the fact that the GP is on duty, and has advertised her presence during her consultation hours in a publicly accessible building, gives people the right to visit her with questions about their health. In so far as she has offered her services like this, then I am saying that the stranger becomes a patient and enters a relationship with the GP upon entering the building. He may of course be turned away, but he first has to be heard *as* a patient.

So the stranger is literally the person I bump into on the street, such that even if I occupy a role elsewhere in my life, I do not bring the role to that encounter, and if I do have any responsibility for that stranger, then it will not be in virtue of that role.

We have already discussed two ways in which I might be responsible for a stranger. First, I suggested that the "responsive doctor" (or nurse, social worker, priest) might consider herself to be on

duty *outside* the hospital or surgery and outside her normal working hours, and therefore available for anyone, not just her allocated
patients, to approach her with their health problems. As such, she
sees herself as serving suffering humanity. For that kind of doctor,
there is perhaps nothing new in this chapter. Second, when I was
discussing the National Health Service in Chapter 2, in the section
"Responsibility for a reckless lifestyle", I described it as involving
a principle of *solidarity* for fellow citizens. Each healthy working
British citizen has effectively consented to being taxed in order to
finance the treatment of sick British citizens. Such an arrangement
is partly justified, but not entirely, by the self-interest behind any
health insurance system. But most of the justification comes from
the presumption of solidarity with other strangers who share British citizenship. Of course, the healthy citizen never needs to *meet*
the sick citizen, let alone treat them: the financing goes through
hospitals and healthcare professionals. But there is enough of a
special relationship with co-nationals to ground a responsibility for
strangers. And this principle of solidarity is one thing that brings
together most identity-conferring groups, chosen and unchosen,
such as ethnic and religious groups, as well as interest groups and
hobby clubs, and to a certain extent the much larger groupings
defined by gender or socio-economic class.[1]

Nevertheless, I want to examine my responsibility to a stranger
with whom I do *not* feel any initial solidarity in terms of shared
group membership, and whom I encounter not through an anony-
mous bureaucracy but face to face.

THE GOOD SAMARITAN

Jesus tells the parable in the Gospel of Luke (10: 25–37). A Jew is
robbed and beaten up, and lies by the side of the road. A priest and
a Levite pass by on the other side. A Samaritan stops, tends his
wounds, takes him to a hotel, and pays for a room. Jesus then tells
his listeners to "go and do likewise".

One of the main messages of the story, at the time of its telling,
is simply anti-tribalist. There was enough of an enmity between
the Jews and the Samaritans that the Samaritan's behaviour would

be taken as extraordinary. In our times, racism has been discredited in the public discourse, in the sense that there are no serious politicians in the West with an *openly* racist agenda (which is not to deny that there is still plenty of racism around). So we are much more inclined to accept the anti-tribalist message as uncontroversial, even if we do not live by it.

But there is more to it than that. The parable implies two points about the *proximity* and *emergency* of another person's needs. There is no duty to seek out emergency needs elsewhere, and there is no duty to tend someone's non-emergency needs, or to tend someone's needs after the emergency has passed (or if they are in more capable hands). Some philosophers, notably Peter Singer,[2] have claimed that the precise physical location of emergency need – whether it is near or far from me – is morally irrelevant, and that I should organize my response depending on whose need is greatest, wherever it is. This would ground a general obligation to transfer non-essential resources to organizations such as charities who make it their business to seek out emergency need all over the world. As a critique of high-consumerist Western culture, Singer's argument is still powerful and important. But there are also two risks associated with such a policy. First, it is too demanding in effectively requiring an extreme material asceticism, and preventing rich Westerners from cultivating any scholarly or artistic or athletic pursuits, for example. Second, it may harm those who have a legitimate claim on my resources, such as members of my family; after all, "Charity begins at home".

The point about emergency needs is a direct challenge to scepticism about the reality of another's suffering. An emergency need is something that is immediately obvious as life-threatening; there is no room for the thought "Does this person really need help?" or the thought "What should I do?", let alone for the thought "What is my duty?" In this sense the parable is a salutary reminder to those contemporary philosophers of mind who, still under the influence of Descartes, claim to be unable to do anything more than *infer* the existence of other people's mental states. Here it is very much relevant that the encounter is face to face – the Samaritan can see, not infer, the suffering directly in the Jew's face.

This leads me to recall the point I made in the previous chapter about the description of the situation as one of a claim and a response, and draw on an argument by Peter Winch in his discussion of the parable in "Who is my Neighbour?" (1987). The Samaritan is presented with a claim, and part of the very recognition of that claim *as* the particular claim it is, and as a claim *on me* here and now, is to respond to the claim. The claim is conceptually linked to the response, without any logical or psychological gap between claim and response. There is no room for the contemplation of a motivationally neutral perception; there is no room for thoughts about duty, or about "my" duty; for thoughts about what people in general ought to do in this situation, or about what the Levite should have done; there is no consciousness of choice, or of weighing reasons for or against. And yet the Samaritan's response is not an unthinking knee-jerk mechanistic reaction; it is very much an intentional, meaningful response (the distinction between reaction and response is important here). All this structure will be best revealed, I suggest, when the waiting BBC reporter corners the Samaritan and asks him why he helped the Jew. The most plausible reaction would be something like "I couldn't just leave him there" – it will *not* be an explanation such as "In situations of this type there are good moral reasons for agents to do their duty by".

The Samaritan's use of the word "couldn't" is important, for it implies a special kind of incapacity, and I will be saying more about this in the next section. For the moment, it should be stressed that I am talking about the phenomenology of the particular encounter between the Samaritan and the Jew; I am not making a banal ethical argument in favour of a duty to help the needy, nor am I chastising the priest and the Levite for failing in their duty: for all we know, they may have passed over to the other side not out of revulsion or scepticism or fear of inconvenience, but because they had any number of good reasons to hurry on to their destination. Part of what it means to have a rich meaningful life is that one has to acknowledge many competing claims on one's time and energy, and occasionally one has to ruthlessly ignore certain otherwise legitimate claims in order to accomplish something.

HUCKLEBERRY FINN

I now want to develop the above ideas by exploring in more detail another example of taking responsibility for a stranger, that of Huckleberry Finn's reluctant protection of the runaway slave Jim in the antebellum American South, from Mark Twain's 1884 book *Huckleberry Finn*. The example is interesting precisely because of the great difference between the two protagonists not only in their age and race, but especially in terms of the racism which Huck can't help feeling towards Jim. Note that the relationship between Huck and Jim could be interpreted as one of friendship, and if that were the case we should speak of the responsibility to a friend, rather than a stranger. However, it is precisely because of Huck's racism that Jim must be a stranger, at least up until the moment when Huck protects him – and that is the moment I want to examine.

Anyway, let us look at the details of the story. Unlike the parable of the Good Samaritan, we have plenty of detail here, and that makes literary works an especially rich source for examples in moral philosophy.[3] Huck is a boy of about thirteen or fourteen years old, living in the American South (the slave state of Missouri) before the Civil War. Huck's mother is dead, his father is an abusive drunkard, and Huck is effectively being raised by an old widow and her sister, Mrs Douglas and Miss Watson. One day Huck decides to run away by faking his own death and hiding on an island in the river. There he meets Jim, an adult slave who belongs to Miss Watson, who has also decided to run away after being threatened with harsher conditions and separation from his wife and children. The two find a raft, and plan to float northwards to the free states, where Jim hopes to earn enough money to buy his family's freedom. Despite the pangs of conscience about helping someone's "property" to escape, Huck agrees to help him.

> Jim said it made him all over trembly and feverish to be so close to freedom. Well, I can tell you it made me all over trembly and feverish, too, to hear him, because I begun to get it through my head that he was most free – and who was to blame for it? Why, me. I couldn't get that out of my conscience, no how nor no way ... It hadn't ever come home to

me, before, what this thing was that I was doing. But now it did; and it stayed with me, and scorched me more and more. I tried to make out to myself that I warn't to blame, because I didn't run Jim off from his rightful owner; but it warn't no use, conscience up and say, every time: "But you knowed he was running for his freedom, and you could a paddled ashore and told somebody." That was so – I couldn't get around that, no way. That was where it pinched. Conscience says to me: "What had poor Miss Watson done to you, that you could see her nigger go off right under your eyes and never say one single word? What did that poor old woman do to you, that you could treat her so mean? ..." I got to feeling so mean and so miserable I most wished I was dead.[4]

It is important to know that Huck never once, either here or in the whole novel, articulates a criticism of the institution of slavery. He never once ceases to consider Jim a slave, and Miss Watson's legitimate property: what he is doing is not only theft, but a personal betrayal as well. And since Jim is a slave, Huck does not consider a promise to him to be as binding as it would be to a white person; nor does he consider a friendship with him to be as significant as with a white person (such as Tom Sawyer).

The main episode that other philosophers and I wish to concentrate on is that with the slave-hunters. Huck and Jim see a light in the darkness, and it comes from another boat. Huck decides to leave Jim on the raft and to paddle over in a dinghy to investigate. At the same time, he has made a resolution: if the occupants of the boat are some sort of authority figures, this will be Huck's chance to turn Jim in. As Huck paddles away from Jim, Jim calls out:

"Pooty soon I'll be a-shout'n' for joy, en I'll say, it's all on accounts o' Huck; I's a free man, en I couldn't ever ben free ef it hadn' ben for Huck; Huck done it. Jim won't ever forgit you, Huck; you's de bes' fren' Jim's ever had; en you's de ONLY fren' ole Jim's got now."

I was paddling off, all in a sweat to tell on him; but when he says this, it seemed to kind of take the tuck all out of me. I went along slow then, and I warn't right down certain whether I was glad I started or whether I warn't. When I was fifty yards off, Jim says:

"Dah you goes, de ole true Huck; de on'y white genlman dat ever kep' his promise to ole Jim."

Well, I just felt sick. But I says, I GOT to do it – I can't get OUT of it.

It turns out that the men in the boat are slave-hunters, with guns, and they are looking for five escaped slaves. This is Huck's opportunity. They ask about the identity of the man over there on the raft, and Huck narrates:

I didn't answer up prompt. I tried to, but the words wouldn't come. I tried, for a second or two, to brace up and out with it, but I warn't man enough – hadn't the spunk of a rabbit. I see I was weakening; so I just give up trying and says – "He's white."

Not only is he white, continues Huck, but he's his father and he's got smallpox and so it would be best if the slave-hunters did not get too close to the raft, and the slave-hunters duly move on. After this episode, Huck feels terrible. This is the last straw after a series of perceived failures. Henceforward, he declares, he will give up on "morals", because he is too weak to follow them; instead he will continue to help Jim, and eventually "go to hell".

Then I thought a minute, and says to myself, hold on – s'pose you'd a done right and give Jim up; would you feel better than what you do now? No, says I, I'd feel bad – I'd feel just the same way I do now. Well, then, says I, what's the use you learning to do right, when it's troublesome to do right and ain't no trouble to do wrong, and the wages is just the same? I was stuck. I couldn't answer that. So I reckoned I wouldn't bother no more about it, but after this always do whichever come handiest at the time.

The novel continues with a series of adventures, but Huck remains friendly and loyal to Jim right to the end, before setting off on his own. There are two philosophical debates surrounding this episode that I want to consider.

The first debate: Bennett v. Goldman

Jonathan Bennett (1974) used Huck as a counter-example to the supposed authority of the "voice of conscience" in moral decision-making. In Huck's case, growing up in a deeply racist society, his own sympathetic feelings for Jim were a more reliable guide, argues Bennett, than the corrupt conventional morality that Huck learned from his surrogate parents and his teachers. We are to admire Huck's sense of responsibility to Jim precisely because of his *irrational* sympathy and *alleged* weakness, and not because of his explicit moral conclusions: there are times when one should follow one's heart rather than one's head.

> The crucial point concerns reasons, which all occur on one side of the conflict. On the side of conscience we have principles, arguments, considerations, ways of looking at things .... On the other side, the side of feeling, we get nothing like that.　　　　　　　　　　(*Ibid.*: 127)

By Chapter XVI we, the readers, have come to trust Huck on this. We are not trusting his *judgement*, however, for he does not *judge* that he ought to lie to the slave-hunters. Rather, we have come to trust his innate but inchoate sense of the good, and we believe that it is this sense that motivates the lie that covers the responsibility he takes for Jim – rather than, say, an inchoate sense of malign mischief or self-interested panic. Clearly, Bennett concludes, there is more to the moral life, and more to what we morally admire, than the agent's determination of the correct propositional judgement. As readers, we not only want to applaud Huck, we want to reassure him that he did the right thing, we want to *give him the words* with which to recognize and endorse the good act he did. Bennett's intuitionist argument fits in with a broader modern liberal conviction that slavery was the result of a particular kind of "moral blindness": we want to believe that many other whites had similar sympathies as Huck, but could not put those sympathies into words strong and clear enough to compete with the dominant racist narrative.

Now, of course Bennett is not suggesting that sympathy should always win out over conscience when the two clash:

> I don't give my sympathies a blank cheque in advance. In a conflict between principle and sympathy, principles ought sometimes to win. For example, I think it was right to take part in the Second World War on the Allied side; there were many ghastly individual incidents which might have led someone to doubt the rightness of his participation in that war; and I think it would have been right for such a person to keep his sympathies in a subordinate place on those occasions, not allowing them to modify his principles in such a way as to make a pacifist of him.
>
> (Bennett 1974: 133)

The answer, concludes Bennett, is that explicit reasons and principles should be regularly tested against, and if necessary adapted to, one's intuitions and sympathies. Often there are good reasons to ignore sympathies, but one should be vigilant to the possibility of cases like Huck which might reveal important defects in the moral reasons and principles that we use for guidance in times of perplexity. The revelation of defects need not imply the wholesale rejection of a community's entire moral structure – most of the moral principles guiding whites living in the antebellum South would be evidently familiar to our own ears.

Bennett's construal of the Huck story as a conflict between conscience and irrational sympathy has been challenged by Alan Goldman (2010). Goldman sees Huck as acting on reasons which are there, in the situation, even though Huck himself does not notice them as such, and could not articulate them as such. For Goldman, the reasons are what *we* (the readers) use to make sense of Huck's taking responsibility for Jim as morally admirable, and to distinguish it from the mere weakness of, say, the reluctant smoker. The reasons are very ordinary ones, having to do with sympathy, friendship, promise-keeping and loyalty.

Even if we are not cognitivists about all emotions, we should recognise that intentional emotions, those directed at persons or objects, represent their objects as having certain properties. They contain implicit judgements, and therefore an implicit awareness of reasons. Sympathy is such an emotion.   (*Ibid.*: 3)

Huck's guiding emotion is sympathy for his friend Jim. Sympathy contains the implicit judgement that a person, typically a person right in front of you, needs help in light of his situation. In Huck's case this emotion is entirely fitting, and its implicit judgement reflects awareness of the reasons to take responsibility for Jim and his longing for freedom. In reflecting such reasons, this is a moral emotion, containing a judgement about the right thing to do, although Huck does not consciously recognize it as such because of his very limited view of what morality requires (*ibid.*: 4).

Indeed, continues Goldman, what Huck did should not be characterized as weakness at all, even though Huck thinks it is. He faced two sets of reasons, even if he could only articulate one set; and he *chose* to go with the better reasons, and this is what we admire him for. Indeed, continues Goldman, lying to the slave-hunters was not an act of weakness but of courage, just as it continued to require courage to stick by Jim when the weak thing would have been to denounce him and avoid the risks of also being punished for colluding with a crime.[5]

The second debate: Williams v. Taylor

Huck's encounter with the slave-hunters could also plausibly be described as an example of "moral incapacity". This was a term coined by Bernard Williams (1995), although he did not use Huck as an example.[6] Williams examines the words "I cannot", and describes three common contexts in which these words might be used uncontroversially: (a) I might be physically unable to do something because of lack of strength or endurance; (b) I might be psychologically unable to do something because I experience an irresistible revulsion or phobia; (c) I might actually mean "I ought not", because the contemplated action would be too immoral, too imprudent or too ugly. But this last category is not a genuine incapacity, says Williams (*ibid*.: 67), since it is perfectly compatible to declare that I ought not do X, and then go on to do X – the phenomenon of weakness of will. With a genuine incapacity, if I go on to do the act then this falsifies my previous declaration that I cannot.

In contrast to all these three meanings, Williams considers the "I cannot" used by Martin Luther in his protest against the Catholic Church: "Here I stand, I can do no other." This is moral incapacity.[7] That this is not a merely psychological incapacity is revealed by the inappropriateness of an observer's suggestion to "try" (*ibid*.: 63). With a phobia, or with the revulsion generated by the prospect of eating roast rat (Williams's example), it will make sense to advise the agent to try, to grit his teeth, or to offer incentives or threats to motivate him further. Perhaps the agent's attempt will be unsuccessful, perhaps not, but either way the incapacity is seen as something external to the self, an obstacle that can in principle be overcome without the self being transformed in the process.

In contrast, if an observer suggested to Luther that he should "try" to compromise with the Catholic Church, this would show that the observer had not understood the nature of Luther's moral incapacity, or was being cruelly cynical. What the incapacity means is that, for the right sorts of reason (i.e. not just bloody-mindedness or political shrewdness), he cannot even try. Indeed, Luther's declaration *presupposes* that he is not physically or psychologically unable to compromise, especially since so many people have already managed to compromise, and there was a general expectation that Luther would too.

Williams offers a second way to distinguish moral incapacity from merely psychological incapacity: the former involves, at least implicitly, some notion of *deliberation*, concluding in the discovery of the incapacity. Luther may or may not have deliberated prior to his declaration, but if he did, we can imagine the sorts of considerations that were running through his mind, and the decisive reasons in favour of protest, reasons that would have made sense to many others at the time regardless of whether they were prepared to join him in protest. With a mere revulsion, there is nothing further that can be said about it other than to further describe the object of the revulsion; in that sense it is morally arbitrary. In contrast, the moral incapacity is essential to the agent's moral perspective on the world and on himself in that world. Here is Williams:

> Of course this does not mean that for every such incapacity that we can rightly ascribe to an agent, he must have deliberated in such terms ... the idea of a possible deliberation by the agent in such terms gives us the best picture of what the incapacity is ... We understand the agent's moral incapacity just because we understand how "I can't" could be the conclusion of his deliberation. (*Ibid.*: 65–6)

We can now imagine Williams speculating about the implied deliberation of Huck's experience of moral incapacity, in a similar way that Goldman speculated about the reasons implied by Huck's experience of his own sympathy. Huck's moral incapacity to denounce Jim to the slave-hunters can only be distinguished from genuine panic or from genuine revulsion precisely according to the deliberation that an idealized Huck *would* undergo if he had the words and the concepts. Williams's position differs from Goldman in that the former considers the reasons generated by the hypothetical deliberation to be *decisive*, leaving the agent no choice. For Goldman, there remain non-decisive reasons for and against, and it is Huck who – admirably – chooses to act on the reasons of friendship, sympathy and loyalty.

Craig Taylor uses the Huck example to criticize Williams.[8] Huck's moral incapacity does not imply any deliberative conclusion about his dispositions and commitments, writes Taylor, but is instead a "primitive fact about him".

> What this example shows is: first, that we might understand an agent's response to be a genuine moral incapacity even though the agent themselves cannot account for it in terms of the kind of reasons suggested above; and second, that in such cases our characterisation of an agent's incapacity as a genuinely moral one turns not on their reasons for action but on the way this and other incapacities for

action are connected to a larger pattern of response in an agent's life, a pattern of response that itself helps to constitute our conception of that agent's character.

(Taylor 2001: 57)

In order to recognize the pattern of response, we have to get to know Huck through the pages of the book. Taylor cites other examples of Huck's compassionate and friendly behaviour towards Jim, and especially the development of Huck's moral consciousness along the journey up the Mississippi river.

As Taylor recognizes (*ibid.*: 64), this would not prevent us from ascribing to him the deliberation that Williams believes must be there in principle. But, asks Taylor, in our conclusion that Huck's incapacity is based on sympathy, we must have *already* formed the judgement that Huck has a sympathetic inclination towards Jim. As such the need for implied deliberation is redundant and comes too late to do any philosophical work in explaining how we make sense of Huck's lie to the slave-hunters. All we need to posit a character trait is Huck as we have come to know him. Taylor's emphasis is very much on the business of reading a literary work: it is *our* response to Huck's response to others that leads us to conclude that he is sympathetic.

THE AGENT'S PERSPECTIVE

I hope that I have provided enough detail about the two overlapping debates, and that the particular disagreements can be kept in mind in what follows. Huck simply finds that he cannot denounce Jim to the slave-hunters and in so doing discovers the content of the responsibility that he had already taken for the stranger Jim after first meeting him. In other words, Huck's responsibility has been tested, and has survived, and indeed been deepened by the encounter with the slave-hunters. The full meaning of prospective responsibility is not only determined by the particular relationship, but also by the events that occur within that relationship through time. Earlier commitments of unconditional responsibility can always be undermined or even falsified in time, partly depending on how the agent or the beneficiary themselves change through time, and depending on the precise challenge posed by the situations they encounter (i.e. situational moral luck).

The two debates above concern the "presence" of reasons, either in the situation (Goldman) or in the agent's mind (Williams), unbeknownst to the agent himself; they also concern the question of how seriously to take the agent's perspective on the matter, both at the moment of wondering what to do, and later, when the agent recalls and evaluates his past behaviour. I want to claim that in both debates, the truth is somewhere between the two extremes.

Bennett and Goldman on reasons in the situation

With regard to the first debate, I think both Bennett's and Goldman's positions are ultimately deficient because the former takes Huck's perspective on the events too seriously and the latter not seriously enough. Bennett sees Huck as too inaccessible to reason, and Goldman sees Huck as too accessible to reason. Bennett does not pay enough attention to the situation in which Huck's action makes sense to us, the readers; Goldman pays too much attention to the situation and ignores the sense it makes (or fails to make) to Huck.

Bennett is too quick to agree with Huck's view of himself as irrational, as motivated by mysterious immoral forces. And yet when Jim on at least three occasions calls Huck his friend, Huck does not *reject* that designation, either to Jim or to others. Even if Huck does not describe Jim as a friend, surely Huck must have noticed the similarity between his feelings for Jim and the feelings he had for an explicit friend such as Tom Sawyer. So this sense of friendship, and the responsibility that would accompany it, is articulate *enough* in Huck's mind. Similarly, Bennett is too quick to accept Huck's declared repudiation of morality: for Huck continues to confidently deploy moral concepts in the remainder of the novel without succumbing to full-grade nihilism, he continues to understand that theft, deception and murder, for example, are wrong, and he continues to refuse to denounce Jim despite this being in his self-interest in many ways. At the same time, Bennett is right that Huck never goes back on his judgement that he had been irrational and weak on that occasion, just as he never comes to morally criticize the institution of slavery that generated his duty to hand Jim over.

On the other hand, Goldman, like all Kantians, is too impressed by the law and by legalistic reasoning as a model for moral responsibility. In the same way that a court assumes that its ultimate description of events is more accurate than the defendant's (i.e. after the defendant has had a chance to defend himself), so too Goldman assumes that his description of Huck's lie carries greater authority than Huck's description. There are no doubt some aspects of morality that function like the law; but not all moral experience can be reduced to the legalistic model without distortion or loss. For example, Kantians have a notorious difficulty dealing with persistent moral disagreement between two equally well-informed and well-meaning parties, neither of whom could be accused of misperceiving the situation and the reasons therein.

So Goldman is prepared to "reassure" Huck that his refusal to denounce Jim is based on the sound moral reasons generated by his situation that he (Goldman) can more reliably articulate than Huck. But there is no essential reason to believe, if Huck and Goldman were in the same room, that Huck *would* listen to Goldman on this subject, or even that he *ought* to; for it is Huck who has to live his own life, who has to decide whom to take responsibility for, and who has to deal with the consequences of taking that responsibility. Goldman might reassure Huck, in the sense of persuade him; but we would not necessarily have to call Huck irrational for rejecting Goldman's reassurance.[9]

In response to this, Goldman would invoke important conventions about reading: part of what it means for us readers to understand this novel *correctly* is for us to see Huck as acting admirably on intelligible reasons of friendship and loyalty, regardless of what Huck thinks. The word "correctly" is important. A racist reader from the antebellum South might agree with Huck that he showed irrationality and weakness in lying to the slave-hunters, and that Huck was indeed colluding in theft and betraying Miss Watson. But, Goldman would say, it is important that this is an *incorrect* reading of the novel, and that it reveals that the racist reader has not understood it, or Huck, properly. However, this response again ignores the perspective of the well-drawn literary character. If we are assuming – as I am for the purposes of this chapter – not only that good literature is continuous with ordinary life, that well-drawn characters have a certain kind of existence independent from their creator and from their readers, and that such characters retain an essential unpredictability, then Huck's view on the matter cannot be as irrelevant as Goldman suggests. For all we know, Huck could continue living long beyond the pages of the novel, and *never* revise his judgement that his lie had been irrational and weak; that possibility has to count for something.

Without Huck's voice, there is a risk of the excesses sometimes attributed by philosophers to psychoanalytic theory. The psychoanalyst can in principle attribute all manner of repressed memories and unconscious desires despite the patient's own memory and experience, and such attributions cannot be falsified by the evidence. The normal response by the psychoanalyst to such scepticism is to remind the philosopher that the psychoanalyst enters into a *conversation* with the patient, a conversation that may well confirm, or overturn, the psychoanalyst's temporary hypotheses about the origins of the present anxiety. In the same way, Goldman's speculation should be taken as the first move in a possible conversation with Huck, rather than as a final, authoritative judgement about which reasons are there and which are not. Ideally, a conversation between any two parties will – in time – reveal the truth, and allow a convergence of each party's opinions on the truth.

Williams and Taylor on the implied presence of deliberation

In terms of the disagreement between Williams and Taylor, my response will be similar: the answer must lie somewhere in between. At the moment of lying to the slave-hunter, Huck does not deliberate; all he does is express the moral incapacity. But Williams says that the only way to distinguish a genuinely moral incapacity from a merely psychological aversion is to posit the deliberative background needed to make sense of the declaration as moral and as admirable. Without such a deliberative background, Huck's lie might have been the result of a non-moral revulsion to the slave-hunter's smell and appearance, say.

Just as I was reluctant to accept Goldman's interest in the reasons implied by Huck's decision, so too am I reluctant to accept Williams's interest in the deliberation that Huck would have carried out if he had had the concepts and the time. But that is not to say that Huck's behaviour was blindly impulsive. There are things other than reasons that could plausibly have appeared in Huck's mind during that crucial conversation with the slave-hunters. One thing might be an *image* of Jim's trusting face, or the *sound* of Jim's voice, saying that Huck was the only friend he had. The responsibility that Huck experiences for Jim might well be associated with, indeed might flow from such non-rational ideas. More elaborately, Huck might have imagined turning Jim in to the slave-hunters, and then having to *face* Jim and *see* his bitter disappointment. Or he might imagine Jim's suffering at the hands of the slave-hunters as they punished him for escaping. None of this imagining requires words or reasons or deliberation.

Huck says to himself: "s'pose you'd a done right and give Jim up; would you feel better than what you do now? No, says I, I'd feel bad." The key word is the *feeling* that Huck is able to imagine. These sorts of sounds, images and feelings all fall short of what Williams would call "deliberation", but I suggest they could still serve to distinguish Huck's incapacity from the merely psychological. When the slave-hunters ask about the identity of the man over there on the raft, Huck might have turned to look at the raft, and to see the man *he* knew to be Jim: that is the moment he would have realized his responsibility not to tell the truth.

In positing a role for the moral imagination here, I am also disagreeing – partly – with Taylor, however. Taylor wants to take Huck's perspective too seriously, and to rule out all kinds of deliberation. Instead, Taylor says, Huck's incapacity can be taken as moral rather than merely psychological *only* because it fits with a larger pattern of behaviour that we see in Huck before and after the incident. Huck has evidently become friendly with Jim by the time of the confrontation with the slave-hunters, and therefore his lie makes sense as an act of responsibility required by this ongoing relationship. That Huck's lie was an act of friendship is then also confirmed in the subsequent development of their relationship.

But this does not seem to determine enough of the meaning of the act. After all, if Huck's lie had in fact been caused only by his revulsion to the slave-hunter's smell and appearance, Taylor would still call it an act of moral incapacity that expressed Huck's friendly feelings for Jim, simply because it *happened* to fit into and cohere with the previous relationship with Jim. Indeed, any number of Huck's unintentional and accidental acts could then be read as expressing and confirming the ongoing friendship. The context of the friendship is certainly important, and Taylor is right to draw attention to it; but it is implausible to claim that it is the single determinant of meaning in the case of *prima facie* ambiguous acts such as Huck's lie.

Once again, the truth would ideally be discoverable through a conversation with Huck after the event. That conversation would still take place within the context of the ongoing friendship, but there would be room for Huck to explore the possible meanings of his act, and for Huck himself to conclude that they might well have been irrelevant or even antithetical to the friendship.

These two debates have admittedly been a bit academic in their complexity, but I hope they have highlighted something about the possible role of reasons, empathy and self-discovery involved when one person takes responsibility for a stranger.

8
LEARNING TO LOVE

In the previous two chapters, I considered what it means to be responsible for and to another person, especially for and to my patient, my child, and a stranger. In this final chapter I want to examine what it might mean to take responsibility for a situation, and indeed to take responsibility for one's future. I have in mind what the individual himself considers a *permanently adverse situation*. Whether or not the situation is permanent, or turns out to be temporary, is beside the point: it is very much the person's viewpoint that matters here, and the rest of his life that he believes will be spent in this adverse situation. I want to argue that there is a kind of taking responsibility which is akin to love, in a sense I shall be careful to define.

Let me start with a couple of examples of permanent adversity:

(1) *The innocent prisoner*. A middle-aged man is sentenced to life in prison for a murder he did not commit. He arrives in the prison, is shown to his cell. There is a bunk with a dirty blanket, a toilet and sink, a table and chair. There is a small window, which he can barely reach with his outstretched hand. There is the heavy door with the spy-hole. "This", the man says to himself, "will be my home. For the rest of my life."

(2) *The disappointed wife*. A young devout Catholic woman meets, falls in love with, and marries a man. Within a few months,

however, she starts to deeply dislike her husband. It is clear to her that he is unlikely to change much. Leaving him, she is certain, is not an option. So how is she going to spend the rest of her life with him?

There are of course plenty of other examples of permanent adversity: developing a permanent chronic illness; giving birth to a child one does not like; being stuck in a bad job because one is too old to start again; loathing a place that one has moved to because of one's spouse's job or family. Indeed, it is characteristic of certain kinds of depression to see one's life as trapped under permanent adversity regardless of the objective conditions of such a life. Of course, in reality the adversity might not be permanent at all, but our protagonists do not know this. To focus my philosophical exploration, however, I will stick to the above two examples, since each of them brings out important aspects of the phenomenon of taking responsibility and learning to love, or at least to try to love; or at least to try to learn to love. What sort of a decision or commitment is this? And how does it reflect on the protagonist?

I have chosen to speak of responsibility and love, rather than acceptance or resignation, for reasons that will become clear. However, I am also picking up on the expression of *amor fati* ("love thy fate") coined by Nietzsche in the *Gay Science*, and then mentioned in other of his works. In *Ecce Homo*, he says:

> My formula for greatness in a human being is *amor fati*: that one wants nothing to be different, not forward, not backward, not in all eternity. Not merely bear what is necessary, still less conceal it – all idealism is mendaciousness in the face of what is necessary – but *love* it.
>
> (Nietzsche 1967: 714)

Indeed, the real test of such a love, for Nietzsche, is the willingness to live the exact same life that one has led, over and over, eternally. Although I think much of what I have to say would be acceptable to Nietzsche, I do not want to get bogged down in the particular Nietzschean terminology and assumptions, and will not mention him or the voluminous secondary literature on him at all.

The important part for me is the word "fate" – that I am fated to endure this adversity for ever – and that nevertheless there is a possibility for me to choose to love it.

I am not sure that it will be possible to elaborate a precise definition of the phenomenon, since I believe it contains a necessary obscurity. As such, I shall be approaching the questions obliquely. I shall start by distinguishing learning to love from a class of expressions which I shall call *making the best*, which is philosophically less problematic.

LOVE AS DISTINCT FROM "MAKING THE BEST OF IT"

Taking responsibility in the sense of learning to love is not "making do" or even "making the best" of a situation, or looking at it "on the bright side", or "gritting one's teeth and bearing it", or "giving the benefit of the doubt". It is not "accepting" or "resigning oneself to it". A woman, though not the one in my example, might choose to remain with her husband as a "lesser evil" than leaving him, perhaps because "better the devil you know". (Although there are important differences between all these expressions, I will speak only of *making the best* for the remainder of this section.) Although making the best may well be a necessary condition for learning to love, there are nevertheless three important differences that I want to explore.

First, making the best is much less philosophically problematic, for it is a matter of temporary selective attention. I can choose to concentrate on the advantageous aspects of the situation; or I can remind myself how much worse it could have been (and indeed has been for others); or I can turn the disadvantages into longer-term advantages by seeing them as character-building, or as providing me with material for a novel. Of course I may be more or less successful at making the best of it; every morning I may have to start again in the face of the renewed awfulness of the situation. But as a survival plan, I think it seems clear enough. In contrast, learning to love is much more philosophically problematic because it seems to involve a decision to *feel* something. Under a popular understanding of the word, love is a passion, something that happens to one upon encountering a particular person or project. If my spontaneous reaction is indifference or hostility, it is hard to see how a mere decision can overcome that, beyond the attempt to ignore it or redescribe it through selective attention and making the best. Now, of course love is much more than just a feeling, and I will have something to say about it in the following section. But for the moment it is enough to note the counterintuitive resonances of "learning to love" and "deciding to love".

Second, making the best therefore has to be an essentially *temporary* project: there has to be not just light at the end of the tunnel, but a conceivable end to the tunnel. When I emerge from the awful situation, either to my fondly remembered previous life, or to a much-anticipated better life, I can start writing the novel. Even if the longing for the end of the tunnel is never actually expressed or thought about, it is presupposed by the very attitude of "making the best". In contrast, the prisoner and the wife, at least in my examples, have accepted that their situation is indeed permanent, that what they are dealing with is the rest of their lives. Of course, their situations may turn out not to be permanent for any number of reasons, but their attitude towards their respective situations is one of no longer hoping or longing for possible ends. Maybe the prisoner does not dare to hope because he fears that his life will be even harder to live after crushing disappointment; maybe the wife cannot imagine leaving her husband because she has come to identify so closely with her role of Catholic wife. But whatever the reasons for their attitude, there is no longer any end to the tunnel in sight.

It is easy to ignore the temporal component of attitudes, that is, it is tempting to see attitudes as something one is "in" here and now, like a suit of clothes, with no essential reference to the future or past. Benevolent or malevolent attitudes to individual people might be an example. But while they might result in identical behaviour, the attitudes of making the best and learning to love differ precisely in the implied temporal location of the protagonist, that is, whether they take themselves to be in the middle of their lives, moving forward to a future that is indeterminate or to a certain extent controllable, or whether they take themselves to be in the "last phase" of their lives, the "rest of their lives", with the future essentially resembling the present.

Of course, my examples might have been different. Another prisoner in the same situation could well hope passively, either by waiting for the miscarriage of justice to be discovered or for an opportunity to escape; or he could hope more actively, either by petitioning and lobbying for a retrial, or by behaving well in the hope of an early parole, or by developing his own escape attempt. And living in hope or fighting for justice can be sources of great strength for people under adversity. But I am interested precisely in that time when the protagonists have *given up hoping*, either because there has not been enough improvement, or because they are more and more worried about growing old and dying with their hopes, about "sulking" away their lives, thereby forgoing any remaining chance that they might have for a modest happiness even under this permanent adversity.

Importantly, however, when I say that the prisoner has given up hope, this does not necessarily mean that he has sunk into despair and despondency (although again, another prisoner in the same situation might well). If he has learned to love his situation – whatever that means – he is somehow steering a course between hope and hopelessness.

Let me just mention one crucial difference between the prisoner's case and the wife's, and that is that the prisoner is physically trapped, whereas the woman – it will be objected – is "only" trapped by convention, religious scruple, pride, and so on; she still has the "physical" choice to leave the marital home and, in most Western jurisdictions, of leaving the marriage. However, what is important in my example is that the woman herself does not see the Catholic prohibition of divorce as a scruple or a convention, but as an absolute against which she cannot even conceive a transgression. To her the prohibitions are as restrictive as prison walls, and she no more chooses her prohibition than the prisoner chooses to be in prison. She may idly fantasize about leaving her husband "if he pushes me too far"; she may say something like "it's so easy for those Protestants"; but the option is not yet a "live" one for her (to use William James's (1979) famous term), precisely because she still identifies so much with her Catholic faith, and with her freely chosen marital status. Again, I stress that any number of things might happen in the future: she may come to lose her faith, or lose

177

enough of it to choose to leave, just as she may reach a point of such despair that she finds she has to leave. But at this moment she cannot seriously imagine reaching that point, and the situation stretches out for the rest of her life.

Making the best differs from learning to love, therefore, first in being less philosophically problematic, and second in being essentially short term. The third way in which making the best differs from learning to love is a bit complicated. Making the best (and the other expressions I listed) essentially involves keeping a certain part of myself logically separate from the awful situation, in a space "behind the lens", whence to judge the situation and plan one's response to it. Learning to love, on the other hand, involves "embracing" the situation and striving to eliminate the distance between the scrutinising self and the scrutinized situation. There is plenty of metaphorical language here to unpack, so let me proceed slowly.

What is distinctive about the attitude of making the best is that the subject remains aware that a "best" needs to be made. In other words, the awful situation before her is not taken as the limits of experience; instead, it is continuously contrasted either with an imagined better situation in the future or with an imagined worse situation in the counterfactual present. In order to resist the awfulness of the real present, the subject has to remind herself, explicitly if necessary, that in being here and now she has moved away from particular unreal alternative situations and towards particular unreal future situations. If a married woman (again, not the woman in my example) considers her situation a "lesser evil", she fixes her attention on the situation as an evil, and invokes the contrast with the alternative, greater evil: for example, life as someone who has broken her marital vows and abandoned her husband, or life as a single divorcée without the husband's income.

Compare this to the Catholic woman in my example; it is not that she has considered the reasons in favour of abandoning her husband, and then rejected the option. The option never occurred to her in the first place as a "live" option, an option into which she could fully immerse herself, far beyond the realm of gratifying daydream. Or perhaps she excitedly entertained the option, both to herself and to friends, perhaps she went through the reasons over and over again, but when it came time to pack the bags she found she could not go through with it; the reasons to leave turned out to be idle. A reason's idleness is not the same as its being outweighed, for she was not actually weighing reasons to herself. Indeed, in further conversation to her bewildered girlfriend she might not be able to offer any reasons that would satisfy either the friend or herself; she is left with the hollow conclusion that she simply "cannot" leave, a statement of moral incapacity.

Now here is the important bit. The awareness, or discovery, that she cannot leave her husband might drive her into despair; or she might grit her teeth and make the best of it. Or, a third option, she might say to herself: "How can I go to bed every night with this man, for the rest of my life, merely to make the best of it? How can I live with a resignation and acceptance that effectively amounts to a pretence? What sort of a life is that?" And she might take responsibility for her life by embracing (that is, choosing to embrace, or rather choosing to try to embrace) the situation, and thereby making it her own, and *reclaiming* her life. Rather than have a life forced on her by circumstances, she retakes the initiative within the circumstances. The circumstances here act as a backdrop, an unchallenged given, against which contrastive characterizations and critical judgements can be made meaningful. I am certainly not suggesting that she become a devoted servant to her husband: embracing the situation, indeed embracing him, is compatible with critical reflection on the aspects of his behaviour and their life together that she can change.

In taking responsibility for her life and embracing the situation, an attitude of genuine love may develop. "Love" here should not be interpreted romantically, that is, as some sort of warm glow that strikes the lover passively. Indeed, the attitude of love resulting from successfully embracing an awful situation need not generate anything beyond a vague contentment with one's lot. Importantly, the loving attitude in question is not primarily to be identified with an affect at all; instead it is a framework of experience built upon a set of evaluative attitudes, a way of making sense of the world and of one's place in it. And like any successful framework, the structure and workings of it will not be fully clear to the subject of that experience. What this phenomenon does share with romantic love, and why I am using the same word for it, is its transformative power. As romantic love bestows value on the beloved,[1] so too will the successful embracing of the awful situation transform it; not transform it into something wonderful, nor indeed something bearable, but transform it into the given.

In the same way that physical embracing eliminates the gap between the lover and the beloved, so too the (attempted) embrace of the situation eliminates (strives to eliminate) the critical distance between the subject and the permanently adverse situation. Embracing the object brings me so close to it that I am no longer aware of where I end and where it begins: I have come to identify with it as mine. This is an important ingredient in leading a life that approaches a kind of integrity, a kind of authenticity, and avoids alienation. The classic discussions of integrity in recent Anglo-American philosophy focus on agents who have a great deal more freedom than the prisoner and the wife, freedom to live one's life according to one's principles and thereby achieve integrity. Jim the botanist in Williams's (Smart & Williams 1973) famous example may decide to intervene in the situation (getting his hands dirty while saving nineteen Indians) or to walk away from it, seeing it as unfortunate but not his problem. But either way the situation is not *his*, and he will have the rest of his life to deal with it in his own way – there is an essential distance between him and his problem, and once he has returned home there are plenty of things to occupy his time and plenty of ways to shape his life. In contrast, I would suggest that the prisoner and the wife are *in* their respective problems, and so cannot achieve the requisite separation; nevertheless, despite being unable to live in accordance with their principles, I believe they can achieve a kind of integrity by learning to love their situations.

Pre-nuptial contracts

This will still be much too metaphorical for many philosophers' tastes, so perhaps it will be helpful to briefly consider another example: the pre-nuptial contract. This will help to bring out the distinction between an essentially first-personal attitude to one's marriage and an essentially third-personal or spectatorial attitude.

"Pre-nups" are legal in some US states, although not in many other countries. The central clause of such a contract will typically run:

> In the event of divorce, each party will assume sole possession of those goods and monies which they brought to the marriage (see list in appendix), and each party will assume possession of one half of those goods and monies created or acquired jointly or severally during the marriage.

Given the divorce statistics in the US and other Western countries, they would seem to make a lot of sense as a form of insurance. However attractive this spouse is to me now, people change in unpredictable ways, and relationships deteriorate even with the best will on both sides. Now, if I knew, based on statistics for my area, that my house had a one in three chance of burning down I would be culpably stupid not to take out insurance. So why have pre-nups not become more popular?

The key is to distinguish between the involved perspective of the spouse and the detached perspective of a spectator. Discussions of rationality (e.g. statistical likelihoods) presuppose an essentially spectatorial perspective: the question is not what *I* should do, but what *anyone* should do in the situation that I happen to find myself in. But such a perspective is incompatible with the trust and commitment that I suggest is necessary for a healthy marriage. A marriage, to be healthy, needs more than rational calculation, for there will be many times when not enough evidence is available to make a decision about the marriage that will satisfy norms of rationality. And trust, like embracing, is an essentially first-personal view of the event, and a half-blind lurching into the future: it is not an attempt to deny or ignore the divorce statistics, but it has to do with a resolve to make the marriage work, that is, with *my* resolve to make *my* marriage work, to believe without naiveté or sentimentality that it is only other people's marriages which fall apart. Taking the rational, spectatorial view of my own marriage implies that it is an experiment that might fail, and one that needs regular re-evaluation to see if conditions are being met; I can make the best of it in the meantime, but already I have laid contingency plans.

This first-personal approach to marriage is by no means unusual. It is shared in sports psychology, career planning workshops and in drug therapy clinics, for example. The only way for some people to finish the marathon or to pass the job interview or to get off the stuff is to *resolve* to win. And my resolve to make my marriage work is fully compatible with the snide remark among the wedding guests: "I'll be curious to see how long this one lasts." And of course they may turn out to be right, just as I may end up being fleeced in the divorce settlement. They may indeed know me better than I know myself, and struggle to withhold those terrible words "I told you so". But none of this undermines the nature of the commitment – not only at the start, but at every moment of crisis – that is required for any sort of genuine, non-instrumental marriage to work in the longer term.

Indeed, it is not just about maximizing the chances that the marriage will work "in the long term", but that it will last "as long as ye both shall live". Taking a marriage seriously means refraining from making *any* provisions for life after the marriage. (The only exception, of course, would be if one's spouse develops a life-threatening illness that provides a palpable time limit.) But the point is that one can only take responsibility for a marriage from within; there comes a point where that is the only perspective that matters, and all offers of advice and warnings from outside, however justified by evidence, are ultimately beside the point.

Tim Chappell's objection to collaboration

By distinguishing the engaged from the spectatorial, the public from the personal perspectives, I would also begin to answer the obvious objection that could be raised against both my protagonists as they try to take responsibility for their respective situations. While the prisoner and the wife have not got as much to lose in material terms as the uninsured spouse, they can still lose their dignity and self-respect. The spectatorial objection could then run as follows: surely this "resigned" love is exactly what the prison guard wants the prisoner to think; for it makes the guard's job much easier. And the husband will get away with the impression that he himself does not need to work harder to save the marriage. Such docile forms of love, such a compliant adaptive preference, the spectator concludes, are evidence of a crushed personality, not a liberated one. Tim Chappell articulated this objection even more forcefully: learning to love, he says,

> makes it possible for the oppressed to bear being oppressed (and hence, much easier for their oppressors to go on oppressing them) ... Why *should* they accept their terrible circumstances? Why shouldn't they fight back, try the locks, question the powers and principles that have put them in durance vile? And why should the fact, if it is a fact, that they won't succeed if they fight back, make it any less reasonable to fight?[2]

This objection misses the point precisely because it comes too late for the protagonists of my discussion. I acknowledge that some other prisoner falsely imprisoned would derive solace and meaning, even from a doomed fight to clear his name. But it is important that the prisoner of my example is worried about "wasting" the remainder of his life in such a futile exercise, however noble it will seem to Chappell. Chappell could accept that "my" prisoner has given up, but still argue that he *should* continue the fight. In response to this, I have to stress that it is ultimately the *prisoner's* life we are talking about, not Chappell's, and that it is the *rest* of the prisoner's life, not a temporary episode. These two facts give his judgement a special kind of authority, not only about the futility of the fight, but also about the reasonability of devoting his life to such a fight. If Chappell walks away, shaking his head and muttering about the prisoner's lack of reasonableness, this response need not concern the prisoner at all.

Chappell later extrapolates from this situation, asking: "How did people cope under Stalin? Precisely by keeping their minds inviolate from the horror and the lies and the institutionalised brutality and stupidity that was all around them." It is certain that *some* people heroically kept their minds inviolate under Stalin, and we certainly admire them for it. The question is whether we should be as impatient as Chappell is with those – the vast majority of Soviet citizens, I would guess – who reluctantly collaborated because they wanted to avoid the even greater horror of a prison camp, or because they wanted to keep a half-meaningful job rather than being allocated tedious manual labour as punishment for dissent, or because they wanted their children to have a chance at going to university. In suggesting that the Soviet citizen can legitimately learn to love their situation, I am not at all saying that they should learn to love Stalin; rather, it is about finding sources of meaning *and of joy* in an otherwise highly depressing situation, a situation that – I repeat again and again – seems permanent.

With regard to the Catholic wife, it is less clear that her situation is one of injustice rather than bad luck. Without clear injustice, it is less clear what it would mean for her to "fight" the situation. But remember: divorce is not an option for her. She will come home to this house every day, and will spend the evenings and weekends with this man. Chappell says (I paraphrase somewhat here): "The first essential for her is never to lose her grip on who she really is – a woman who hoped for a loving marriage. It would be better to die without losing that grip than to adapt in the way Cowley suggests." So either Chappell is recommending suicide to her, or he is recommending that she cling to an image of "what she really is" *for the rest of her life*: she lives with a man in a single house, shares his bed, but is to grit her teeth and tell herself over and over "This is not who I really am", recounting her hopes for a loving marriage over and over, and cursing cruel fate for ruining things for her. Surely this is a classic example of the tyranny of the past over the present, and of an irresponsible evasion of the present and future?[3]

CAN LOVE BE COMMANDED?

Even if we can accept the difference between making the best and learning to love one's situation, what can it mean to decide to love, or to decide to learn to love? I have said something in terms of embracing the situation, but in this section I want to look at a partial analogy, that of trying to learn to love a piece of music.

I cannot decide to love Beethoven's *Fidelio* here and now if I do not spontaneously do so already, that much is clear. But there are things I can do that will increase the chances that I will come to love it in time. For a start, I can decide to listen to it a second time, and a third, perhaps upon the advice of a friend to suspend judgement. I can decide to listen to it more closely, "especially to this bit" (advises my friend), and so on. Indeed, my friend's enthusiasm might prove infectious on its own.

Second, I can decide to take a music appreciation class, where an expert will tell me and show me what to look for in attending to *Fidelio*. This might involve some systematic teaching in music theory, or in musical history, or in Beethoven's biography. It would almost certainly involve studying the lyrics closely, understanding their meaning and their dramatic import, studying the plot and the characters, watching the performance as well as listening to it. It might involve an introduction to easier, more melodious pieces of opera first, to lay the ground for the more difficult *Fidelio*. In summary, there is a language of musical appreciation that the student needs to learn before a discussion of *Fidelio*'s qualities can take place; and control of the language develops hand in hand with the cognitive development, that is, the ability to hear what is there below the surface. Of course, the process offers no guarantees that the student will come to actually love the piece, or that he will even come to appreciate it. But if the course is a success, then it would be correct to say (a) that the student decided to take the course; (b) that he intended to improve his appreciation of music, to deepen his enjoyment, and to widen the repertoire of pieces he loves; (c) that he came to love the piece because of his taking the course; and (d) that he was *missing something* (something that was there all along) in his initial dislike of the piece.

But this analogy with my two examples fails, for two interrelated and revealing reasons. First, there is a relatively uncontroversial canon of musical works that it can be plausibly said that people should appreciate, even if their unlearned ear rejects them. There is also a relatively uncontroversial process by which one can develop a more sophisticated musical ear, can learn to discover features of the music that were hidden before, and indeed there is a process by which one can learn to become a recognized expert in musical history or theory oneself, where an expert by definition is someone whose authoritative opinion should be listened to. None of this applies to the prison or the marriage, however.

185

Second, as we saw in my discussion of pre-nuptial contracts, the sort of love I am investigating is essentially personal. This means that the prisoner's judgement about what ought to be done carries a special authority in virtue of pertaining to his own life. Learning to love *Fidelio* cannot achieve such importance, cannot fill a life in the same way as the prisoner's learning to love the prison. (Perhaps the situation will be more complicated for a virtuoso musician, but neither of our protagonists is that.) Moreover, there is not the same notion of surface and depth in my examples. With Beethoven, it makes sense to say that the lovable features are already there, below the surface, ready to be discovered with a little guided digging. But the prisoner and the wife already know everything relevant to the awfulness of the situation: there is nothing new that anybody could show them, let alone a putative expert. Even if a close friend reminds the wife that "Things could be worse", this is not at all the same thing as saying, "Listen to it again, and concentrate on the fourth bar". And the friend, while he may know the wife very well, does not have the same *general* authority that comes from expertise built on training, knowledge and experience in a subject.

Indeed, because taking responsibility for a bad and permanent adverse situation is such a personal process, it is very hard to say anything general about it; there is an essential obscurity to it, akin to a religious conversion. (In fact, learning to love God might be one way to love the situation, that is, coming to see the situation as required by God's inscrutable will.) So here is another analogy that might help us to understand, although again there will be limits to the analogy. The religious conversion involves the doubter somehow opening his heart to the real possibility that God exists, rather than opening his mind to reasons and persuasion. It is a "leap of faith", which flies in the face of the lack of evidence. Indeed, all the ingenious "proofs" typically offered by theist philosophers through the ages (e.g. the ontological and cosmological arguments) are irrelevant to the business of actually acquiring faith. One cannot decide to believe at a merely intellectual level; but there nevertheless can be a decision at a deeper level, the willingness to accept the experience *as* a religious one, rather than to reach for debunking or deflationary explanations.

The leap of faith is a form of embracing, as I described the term in the previous section, and the leap involves the same risks of embracing. In embracing his situation, the prisoner invites the accusation that he is colluding with injustice and abandoning self-respect. In leaping into faith, the doubter invites the accusation of wilfully deluding himself with false consolations, without evidential support.

However, there remains an important difference between the religious conversion and any non-religious learning to love, and that is that the former is likely to bring one into a *community* of worshippers with a common language, common reference points and common understandings. One can discuss one's dilemma with the priest, and receive relevant advice in theological terms. In so far as the religious conversion can be assisted by taking part in the religious community as a doubter, then it will begin to resemble the case of learning to love *Fidelio* and thereby slowly acquiring membership in the community of music lovers. On the other hand, the prisoner and the wife in my examples remain utterly alone in their respective situations. If they have friends to confide in, the advice of such friends can carry no authority beyond compassion. Indeed, it is not clear the degree to which the wife *can* confide in a friend precisely because the friend has not had to learn to love that particular man.[4] If the friend disagrees with the wife's decision to learn to love, then she will not be able to express her disagreement any more; if she agrees with the wife's decision, then it will have become something unmentionable as a decision in the past or as a project in the present. It is not as if the friend can invite the wife to take a more objective stance on her husband by asking "So how's the learning to love coming along, then?" Both the decision, and the subsequent efforts, remain personal in this deep sense, and can only be carried forward by the agent's own will.

To conclude this section in a way that will strike many as lame, I am suggesting that yes, love can be commanded, indirectly. Part of the process will be like making the best, that is, a concerted process of selective attention. Part of the process will be like the religious conversion, with the leap of faith and the opening of one's heart to the possibility of love. But there will always be an irreducible component of luck involved: of two prisoners in the same situation, one might manage to learn to love that situation, the other might not. As such we might be back in the mire of the problem of moral luck (see Chapter 5). However, again we have to be cautious about the perspective on the situation. In comparing one person's lucky success (in taking responsibility for his situation) with another's unlucky failure, we are adopting Nagel's third-personal comparative perspective. But the agent might not be interested at all in the lucky success of some real or hypothetical other person – all that interests him are his own efforts; the prisoner is alone in his cell and alone in his situation. Second, the agent may not even see his own failed efforts in terms of bad luck; he might see them as simply a temporary setback requiring renewed efforts, in a spirit of "try, try again" and "whatever it takes". It is not clear what our two agents would achieve by conceiving of their situation, or their efforts to deal with that situation, in terms of good or bad luck.

THE PROBLEM OF SELF-DECEPTION

Over much of the above discussion hangs the spectre of self-deception.[5] Perhaps greater than the prisoner's risk of colluding with injustice, greater than the Catholic wife's risk of self-denigration, greater than the religious convert's risk of being engulfed by the religious community, lies the risk of self-deception. Surely the best way of dealing with a bad situation is to start by being honest about it and about one's spontaneous feelings towards it. This is not the same as saying that one's feelings cannot be wrong, for there is always room for reflecting on whether those feelings are appropriate. But in order to reflect on those feelings one needs to know as much as possible about the situation that one is facing.

In contrast, I have been suggesting that the prisoner and the woman may be able to learn to love their situations, and that this can be philosophically legitimate. At the same time I am not denying the awfulness of the situations they find themselves in: not only the prison environment, of course, but the bad luck and injustice that put the prisoner there. With the marriage, it is tempting to say that "It can't be that bad", especially since I have deliberately avoided an example involving the objective wrong of physical abuse.[6] However, it should be remembered that we are talking

188

about a marriage, that is, a degree of sustained intimacy – sexual and domestic – that the wife does not share with anyone else, including the closest members of her family. At work the wife can get along with an annoying colleague because she has her own desk, her own job description, and her own working hours that come to an end at 5pm; in short, she has her own space, her own privacy. But it is this sense of private space that is directly under threat from marital friction, a space further constricted by the weariness of pretence and the bitterness of disappointment.

One response to this objection would be to say that the prisoner and the wife are indeed engaged in self-deception, but that it is justified and not blameworthy. In fact, I will eventually be arguing that learning to love is not self-deception, but before I can do that I have to say more about paradigmatic examples of self-deception.

The notion of non-blameworthy self-deception is sometimes called the "vital lie" – the sort of self-deception that some people need to attempt just to get on in life at all. For here what is at stake is a very real truth, but one that would paralyse the subject if faced squarely. There are certain facts that the tightrope-walker would be wise not to contemplate until he returned to solid ground, and nobody would blame him for his avoidance. The low self-esteem of the recovering alcoholic requires a systematic programme of self-praise and self-encouragement until he manages to rid himself of temptation. But there is one thing about the vital lie that makes it more akin to making the best than to learning to love, and that is its essentially short-term nature – and this is important for the indulgence we accord the vital lie. Temporary but justifiable self-deception should either result in cure, or in the decision to try a different form of "treatment" before the patient loses too much contact with reality. The concept doing the work here is that of justification, and justification has a forward-looking aspect, as when we say that the end justifies the means, and the proof of the pudding is in the eating.

But it is important to see that the concept of justification is also essentially spectatorial, and has to take place in the public space of reasons. When someone says "I can justify it to myself", they are not using the concept in the full philosophical sense *until* they are able to justify it to others, that is, until others have accepted the justification. Anything less than that will be rationalization, that is, a species of philosophically illegitimate self-deception. When we say that the vital lie is justified, then *either* we are speaking about the term used by those treating the drug addict, *or* we are speaking about the term when used by the drug addict himself, once he is cured, as he looks back on the vital lie. In other words, if the vital lie – and indeed any other kind of paternalistic enticement or restriction – is justified, then it will be seen to be justified by any rational spectator, including the agent once he no longer needs to engage in it.

The essentially spectatorial perspective presupposed by the self-deception involved in the vital lie is what distinguishes it from learning to love. And so I am not trying to say that learning to love is a justified form of self-deception, even though, from the inside, the two experiences might be similar. That leaves me with the second possible response, that learning to love need not involve self-deception at all. It may involve it, of course: all decisions are vulnerable to self-deception, but it need not.

In order to get a handle on this, it will be useful to take a paradigm case of normal *other*-deception: the corrupt used-car salesman and the gullible buyer. Here there is a clear role for the truth about the state of the car: the salesman knows the truth, and conceals that knowledge in order to sell it at a higher price; the buyer is ignorant of that truth, trusts the salesman and loses money. We would be inclined to blame the salesman for his dishonesty, but perhaps also to blame the buyer (to a lesser degree) for misplacing his trust. But when the deceiver and the deceived are the same person, then it is hard to see in what relationship the self-deceiver stands to the truth: if she knows the truth, than she cannot be deceived about it; if she does not know the truth, then she cannot deceive herself about it. I do not want to get bogged down in the answer here, but there will be something to do with selective attention and different levels of knowledge.

Let us now consider a paradigmatic example of *self*-deception: the infatuated teenager. He claims that "This time, she really is my true love". His friend has heard this too many times before, knows him too well, and responds: "Don't deceive yourself, this is just another infatuation." The teenager sincerely believes that it is love, but the situation is clearer to the friend in virtue of his greater distance from the object of affection, and of his knowledge of the adolescent's past behaviour in similar situations. Here it makes sense to say that this self-deception is bad, that it is something the teenager himself will – in principle, and barring plausible explanations for failure – come to regret in the future, and that any action taken by the friend to hinder the teenager's aberrant urges would be justified. But more importantly, the accusation makes sense because it is clear that the teenager is the same person throughout: before meeting the girl, after becoming infatuated with the girl, and after realizing that what he felt was infatuation. It is against the background of who the teenager is and remains (and is known to be by the friend) that the accusation makes sense. The friend assumes that the teenager is sufficiently self-honest in most other important areas of his life that he will, eventually, come to recognize the self-deception for what it is.

The question now is whether this paradigm can fit the case of the prisoner and the wife who genuinely learn to love their respective situations, and I want to suggest it does not, and give two familiar reasons. First, again, the timeframe is of crucial importance. The teenager's self-deception is essentially temporary; whether or not he is in fact deceiving himself is something that will in principle soon be revealed. If, despite expectations, the teenager continues to claim to love the girl, marries her, and stays with her for fifty years, then at some point during that marriage the doubters will have to admit that they are wrong. Does it even make sense for the doubter to claim that the former teenager, now of course a pensioner, has been deceiving himself *for his whole life*? After all, infatuation is also time-limited; one cannot be infatuated – this is what the doubter is accusing the teenager of – for more than a few weeks or months. And if the teenager-pensioner has been deceiving himself for other reasons, then this will beg a much more complicated explanation for his behaviour.

As with all claims about another person's mental states, it is important to place the question of self-deception within the context of an explicit accusation by the doubter, rather than asking whether X is deceiving himself, full stop. Consider another example: my brother asks me for a loan and I refuse him. My wife accuses me of being stingy. I respond, "You're wrong, I refused him the loan because he's always frittering away money and he should learn to manage his affairs." She then accuses me of self-deception to cover up my stinginess. Stung by this, and knowing her to be a good judge of character, I sit down and explore my own motives, I reflect on my other beliefs and behaviour, and do not find them inconsistent; I come to the conclusion that I am not stingy, that I really am think-ing of his longer-term well-being. Of course I could be wrong, since I can always be wrong about my own motives – only time will tell. I may well come to a different conclusion next week or next month; I may well be forced to come to a different conclusion after repeated argument and behavioural evidence from my wife. But until I come to a different conclusion, then I have come to *this* conclusion, that I am genuinely motivated by concern for his interests. I tell my wife this, and in an important sense, I have seen off the accusation of self-deception, even if I have not convinced my wife. There is noth-ing more to say, at least not for the moment. For this particular disagreement is not akin to disagreements about matters of verifi-able objective fact, where she can lead me by the hand to prove me wrong about the crookedness of the door I just mounted upstairs, or where she can lead me to a dentist to prove me wrong about the seriousness of the pain in my tooth.

The second important difference between the teenager and our two examples has to do with this notion of transformation. The teenager who soon admits that he was self-deceived clearly remains the same person throughout. But there is a very real sense in which the wife and the prisoner have become different people precisely because they have learned to love that which they ini-tially abhorred. The transformation of them as people reflects the transformation of the prison and the marriage, hitherto so abhor-rent, to actual objects of love. Because the prisoner and the wife have embraced their situations, their situations are part of their new identities, and allow them to assume a new integrity, and cor-respondingly a new dignity. Moreover, they are substantial parts of their new identities. The teenager's infatuation was never more than a hobby to fill the boredom. In contemplating the prison and the marriage, the prisoner and the wife are contemplating a major part of their present lives, and a major part of the rest of their lives.

I have to be careful about the language of transformation. In terms of the usual philosophical debates about personal identity, obviously the prisoner remains the same person throughout, both in the bodily criterion and the psychological criterion. Obviously he would not deny moral responsibility for all the things that he remembers doing before he got to prison. At the same time, taking responsibility for one's situation in the way I have been describing entails transforming the relevant background structures of meaning in the prisoner's life. In now accusing the prisoner of self-deception, the accuser would be drawing on the prisoner's pre-imprisonment background structures of meaning for the accusation to make sense. But since the background structures have been transformed, the accusation can no longer be accepted by the prisoner. Importantly, the prisoner's inability here is not a contingent and irresponsible psychological reluctance (as in the reluctance to hear bad news or carry out an unpleasant duty), but rather a conceptual inability.

CONCLUSION

We have come a long way in this book, probably too long a way for a book of this length. Even with all the business I decided to omit (free will, insanity, politics), moral responsibility is still a hugely rich and variegated concept, with so many implications for our understanding of what it means to live a human life. Or at least, that is what I hoped to show. I began with what has been of most interest to philosophers and lawyers, namely the individual's responsibility for a discrete act, and the various ways that others can evaluate and respond to that responsibility. I then moved on to this broader notion of prospective responsibility for a patient, a stranger and, more abstractly, for a situation and for one's life. I believe that the concept is still sufficiently unified to write a single book on it, and that many of the components of retrospective responsibility are, upon closer examination, relevant to the prospective orientation. But in order to see the unity, one first has to challenge some dominant metaphysical assumptions shared by both philosophers and laypeople alike: for example, the pastness of the past, the self-contained nature of the individual's mental life, and the discreteness of choice. All of these challenges could only be adumbrated, and would need more elaborate defence. Finally, the unity of the concept requires a better understanding of three dichotomies that have been running throughout the book: the subjective–objective dichotomy, the active–passive dichotomy captured in the notion of a response, and the personal–impersonal dichotomy; although they overlap, and are often confused one for the other, they are not identical. I believe that there is an eliminable tension at the heart of all three dichotomies, one that relates intimately with the human condition.

NOTES

INTRODUCTION

1. "It is the time you have lost with your rose that makes your rose so important."

   "It is the time I have lost for my rose …," said the little prince, in order to remember.

   "This truth has been forgotten," said the fox. "But you must not forget it. You become responsible, forever, for what you have tamed. You are responsible for your rose …"

   "I am responsible for my rose," the little prince repeated, in order to remember.

2. Compare the German word *verantwortlich*, which is related to the word *Antwort* (an answer). So the person, in so far as they are held responsible, owes the accuser an answer. In English there is the word "answerable", but this seems to relate more tightly to institutional superiors.

3. I am borrowing the terms "retrospective" and "prospective" from Duff (2005).

4. Antony Duff (2005) calls this type of responsibility *status* responsibility.

5. It is true that at the quantum level the usual deterministic assumptions have to be suspended, and the motion of electrons seems to be essentially random. However, there is still no more room for human free will in a universe which is fundamentally chaotic as there is in a universe that is fundamentally determined.

6. The best place to start is the online *Stanford Encyclopedia of Philosophy* (http://plato.stanford.edu), and Timothy O'Connor's entry on "Free Will" and Andrew Eshelman's entry on "Moral Responsibility" (accessed September 2013). Elinor Mason (2005) also provides a useful survey. The most important investigations into the compatibility of free will and moral

responsibility are those of Fischer & Ravizza (1999) and Dennett (1984).

7. The classic account of Nazi machinery remains Hannah Arendt's [1962] 2011 *Eichmann in Jerusalem: A Report on the Banality of Evil*.

8. The case reference is 8 ER 718, [1843] UKHL J16, and the full text is available at: www.bailii.org/uk/cases/UKHL/1843/J16.html (accessed September 2013).

9. A good starting place for discussions of mental illness is Joel Feinberg (1970).

10. One popular example in the literature surrounding moral dilemmas is that of Sophie from William Styron's 1979 novel *Sophie's Choice*. Once inside a concentration camp, Sophie is forced to choose which of her two children will live and which will die. Several of the articles in Mason (1996) discuss the example.

11. A runaway train carriage (the "trolley") will either continue down its present line, thereby killing five railway engineers, or it can be diverted onto a siding where it will only kill one engineer. You control the points. What should you do? And either way, how responsible would you be for the outcome? See Foot (1977).

12. Judith Thomson (1971) argues for the moral permissibility of abortion in cases of rape. A woman is kidnapped, and when she wakes up, she is chained to a bed with various tubes coming out of her body. It turns out that a famous violinist (therefore a great artist and useful member of society) is on the bed next to hers, in a deep coma. Her kidneys are necessary, it seems, for his survival and recovery. However, the procedure will only last nine months, after which she is free to leave. Thomson side-steps the intractable debate over the moral status of the foetus, and argues that although it would be very "nice" for the woman to agree to the procedure, we cannot say that she has a responsibility to the violinist.

13. The teletransporter comes from the original 1970s *Star Trek* television series. A person steps into the transporter in one place, his precise substance is "read" by a machine, and the substance dissolved. The information is then transmitted to another place, where the transporter assembles *new* substance into a perfect replica of the original person. In terms of the person's experience, he enters place A and then appears instantaneously in place B, and he has exactly the same psychological states, especially his memories. The philosophical question is whether it is the *same* person or not, and whether the post-transporter, reassembled person is responsible for, say, a crime committed by the pre-transporter person. See Parfit (1984).

14. Jim is a botanist working in a South American jungle in a politically turbulent state. He stumbles across a group of Indians who are to be executed by firing squad by state soldiers. The head soldier, as a cruel joke, invites Jim to shoot one of the Indians himself, and as an incentive offers to release the remaining Indians. See Williams's section of Smart and Williams (1973).

1. DEFINING RETROSPECTIVE RESPONSIBILITY

1. In most textbooks these are called the "conditions" or "criteria" of moral responsibility. I prefer the word "assumption" to stress the observer's perspective in making the accusation, and the location of the accusation within a two-person relationship. Conditions and criteria suggest a fact of the matter about whether the person is or is not responsible.

2. The Control assumption is sometimes described in terms of the existence of "alternative possibilities" available to but unchosen by the agent. If the agent can show that no other possibilities were in fact open to him, then he did not have control and he was not morally responsible. In a famous 1969 paper, "Alternate Possibilities and Moral Responsibility", Harry Frankfurt denied that alternate possibilities were necessary for responsibility attributions *if* the possibilities were not available but the agent genuinely believed that they were available. For example, I am driving with a companion in that companion's car, and unbeknownst to me the car is a driving instruction car with a second set of pedals which I do not notice. I might genuinely believe myself to have the possibility to drive at high speed, but the companion is worried, and is ready to disengage my accelerator and apply his brake when necessary. As it happens, I have no desire to speed, and drive cautiously all the way home. I believe I was free to accelerate, but in fact I was not since the worried companion would have braked. Nevertheless, Frankfurt claims that I still acted freely and chose to drive cautiously. The article has been reprinted in the anthology *The Importance of What We Care About: Philosophical Essays* (Frankfurt 1988), which contains a number of classic articles relating to moral responsibility.

3. For a classic survey of different kinds of excuses, see Austin (1956).

4. For a much more detailed discussion of the many types of ignorance, see Sher (2009). Sher criticises what he calls the "searchlight view" of moral responsibility, according to which one can only be held responsible for the information "lit up" by one's searchlight of knowledge or attention.

5. I am drawing on the English case of *R. v. Ahluwalia* [1992] 4 All ER 889. For more on this type of case see Stocker (1999).

6. The recognition of diminished responsibility in such a case is something relatively new. An important predecessor took place fifty years earlier: *R. v. Duffy* [1949] 1 All ER 932. A battered woman killed her husband in his sleep, and was charged with murder. Her argument that she had been provoked was rejected by the judge on the grounds that she had not undergone any sudden and temporary loss of self-control. The jury responded to her plight by recommending mercy, with the result that her death sentence was commuted to life imprisonment (from which she was released after three years).

7. It is worth noting that in Anglo-American jurisdictions, duress cannot be a defence for murder. That is, the law effectively states that when someone is trying to get you to murder a third party, then you are supposed to resist even at the very real risk to your life. (Without such a proviso, the Mafia would get innocent third parties to do all their dirty work for them.)

8. Section 55 sub-section 6(c).

9. *R v. Clinton (Jon-Jacques)* [2012] EWCA Crim 2.

2. RESPONSIBILITY FOR MISTAKES

1. Car insurance is a bit more complicated because of the very real danger of harming others through reckless driving. Here it makes sense for the state to impose compulsory second-party insurance, but to leave first-party insurance up to the car-owner.
2. *Hyam* v. *DPP* (1975) AC 55.
3. This was confirmed in the legal case of *R* v. *Cunningham* [1982] AC 566, where the defendant smashed a bar stool over the victim's head several times, resulting in skull fractures and haemorrhaging from which the victim died a week later.
4. *R.* v. *Nedrick* (1986) 8 Cr. App. R. (S.) 179. Once again, the defendant claimed that he had only been trying to scare or punish the victim, and had not intended to kill the baby that ended up dying in the house fire. The appeal was granted.
5. *R.* v. *Caldwell* [1981] 1 All ER 961.
6. The modern classic on the doctrine of double effect is Philippa Foot's "Abortion and the Doctrine of Double-effect" (Foot 1977).
7. See the Department for Education's web section on "School Attendance", and especially the sub-page on "Revised regulations on education-related penalty notices": www.education.gov.uk/schools/pupilsupport/behaviour/attendance/a00208166/penalty-notices (accessed September 2013).
8. This is the thesis in Michelle Moody-Adams's excellent article "On the Old Saw that Character is Destiny" (1993). The volume it is in contains a number of other good essays about character.
9. Susan Wolf calls this the "real self" view of responsibility, a view she ultimately seeks to reject in favour of the voluntaristic account. See chapter 2 of Wolf (1993). For a detailed response to Wolf, see Smith (2008). The original idea of the real self view goes back to David Hume's *Treatise Concerning Human Nature*, Part III, ch. 1. On Hume's account, see Kinnaman (2005).

3. APOLOGY AND FORGIVENESS

1. This section draws on Pettigrove & Collins (2011). Unlike me, they conclude that it is possible to apologize for one's character, although they aim to show that the standard act-based account of apologies (e.g. Smith's account) has to be modified to accommodate apologies for character traits.
2. Perhaps the most famous conditional account is that of Jeffrie Murphy, in Murphy & Hampton (1990).
3. The term "offender" comes from my schematic case, not from Garrard & McNaughton.
4. Derrida's writings are notoriously difficult, and I do not have the space or the expertise to go into them any further in this book. It will suffice for my purposes to explore this one insight.

4. PUNISHMENT

1. Tim Chappell, in his comments on an earlier draft, asked why the institutional relationship was necessary. Imagine two neighbours, one of whom owns a dog, and allows it to go into the other neighbour's garden to dig up the flowers. What is to prevent the flower-owner from "punishing" the dog-owner by leaving poisoned meat out for the dog? In response, I would call that "revenge" or "deterrence", rather than punishment, precisely because of the lack of institutional authority, and the lack of a crime as previously defined by that authority. The flower-owner is merely using the poisoned meat as a means to manipulate the behaviour of the dog-owner.

2. This is the phrase first used in the English Bill of Rights of 1689, then imported into the Eighth Amendment of the American Constitution.

3. This is the line taken in a striking defence of retributivism by Mabbott (1939), – which is still worth reading today.

4. Immanuel Kant is famous for the following: "Even if a civil society were to be dissolved by the consent of all its members (e.g., if a people inhabiting an island decided to separate and disperse throughout the world), the last murderer remaining in prison would first have to be executed, so that each has done to him what his deeds deserve and blood guilt does not cling to the people for not having insisted upon this punishment; for otherwise the people can be regarded as collaborators in his public violation of justice." (Kant, *The Metaphysics of Morals*, 6: 333).

5. There is an interesting path of philosophical influence here. Hampton's theory develops the insights from Feinberg (1965). Hampton herself then influenced Antony Duff's "communicative" theory of punishment: see Duff (2000).

6. *R. v. Sussex Justices, ex parte McCarthy* [1924] 1 K.B. 256 at 259, High Court (King's Bench) (England & Wales).

7. The fates of two other Nazi war criminals are interesting to compare to Eichmann's in this regard. Hermann Goering was Hitler's deputy for many of the Nazi years, was caught after the war, and sentenced to death by the Nuremburg Tribunal. As a life-long soldier, he was not troubled by the execution, but he was troubled by the prospect of hanging, which he considered dishonourable – he believed a soldier should die by a firing squad. In the end he committed suicide by a smuggled cyanide capsule, and there was a widespread sense that he had got away unpunished, a belief that a consequentialist could not understand. Albert Speer was in charge of the Nazi slave labour programme during the latter half of the war, and was sentenced by the Nuremburg Tribunals to twenty years in prison, which he duly served. During those years he wrote two autobiographies, published in English translation in 1970 as *Inside the Third Reich* and in 1976 as *Spandau: the Secret Diaries*. The autobiographies provide a striking testimony of the author's sincere effort to understand what he had done, and why he had done it; but it falls far short of full remorse, a remorse which may have been psychologically impossible without going mad.

8. Abdulbaset Ali Al Megrahi, an employee of Libyan airlines, was sentenced

in 2001 to life imprisonment by Scottish judges for the 1988 bombing of a Pan Am flight over Lockerbie, Scotland, resulting in the death of all 270 passengers and crew. In 2009 he was diagnosed by Scottish doctors with terminal prostate cancer and given three months to live. According to the official statement, this was the reason he was then released to Libya. (Suspicions of other motives in play were confirmed when he lived through to the spring of 2012.)

5. MORAL LUCK

1. The best anthology on the problem of moral luck Statman (1993), which begins with the revised versions of Williams's and Nagel's papers. It also contains an excellent introductory summary of the problem, and an interesting postscript by Williams.
2. Nagel actually compares two Germans (1979: 26), but I want to avoid the particular problems of trying to understand the relationship that ordinary Germans had with the Nazi party. It is much more plausible to say that a Frenchman's collaboration with the Nazi occupation forces was motivated purely by self-interest and not by enthusiasm for Nazi ideology or German greatness.
3. Brooke Barnum-Roberts (2011) considers the analogous situation of a person who wants to apologize for wronging someone, but does not regret it because, from his present perspective, he considers his life to have been considerably improved by the educational value of that wrongdoing. Her example is that of a reformed offender.
4. "Wrongful life" suits should be distinguished from "wrongful birth" suits; in the latter, it is the *parent* who is suing the hospital for the financial and psychological costs of the pregnancy and birth. A "Wrongful life" is brought about by the *child*.
5. *Curlender v. Bio-Science Laboratories*, 106 Cal. App. 3d 811 (1980).
6. I am thinking of Kathryn Bigelow, famous for being the first woman to win an Academy Award for best director in 2009. But in my discussion I do not want to be bound to the particular details of her biography.
7. For a famous disagreement with my position here, see Saul Kripke's (1980: 77) argument that Aristotle could have decided not to study philosophy.
8. Joel Feinberg (1995) is so troubled by the two assassins case that he proposes changing the homicide law so as to merge attempted murder and murder into a single crime, where culpability would be entirely based on intention, regardless of success. He proposes a new offence of "Wrongful Homicidal Behaviour", with a single penalty for conviction.
9. A famous dramatic example of agent-regret is Sophocles's play *Oedipus Rex*. As with the lorry-driver, Oedipus is not to be held responsible for killing his father and marrying his mother, but he clearly feels the particular kind of responsibility Williams calls agent-regret, and his self-blinding gives expression to the shameful transformation brought about by his unwitting acts.

10. Williams's own summary on p. 22 is already semi-fictionalized. Don Levi (1993) discusses moral luck in the context of the real historical figure of Paul Gauguin.

6. ROLE-RESPONSIBILITY

1. I have a friend who is a consultant in emergency medicine, and who has three children. I imagine the fabulous sense of *safety* that those children must have as they grow up. Whatever happens to me, Daddy can deal with it; Daddy has access to all the tools; Daddy can get a helicopter in to pull me out of danger; Daddy knows skilled surgeons who owe him favours. In this sense the mere presence of a doctor, with all his mystical powers and his familiarity with the depths of suffering, can reassure.

2. This sense of a calling might be part of a religious worldview, as it is with many doctors. Serving suffering humanity then becomes a way of serving God. However, this generates two problems not faced by non-believing doctors. First, how to square a belief in the supernatural with the *rigidly* scientistic world of medicine, one that does not allow theology or indeed the humanities any significant room in the modern medical curriculum, for example. Second, the believing doctor will be particularly vulnerable to losing her faith when she witnesses the prolonged suffering of a child.

3. Harry Frankfurt (1998: 9) draws a similar distinction between duty and love, where he construes love much less in terms of a feeling, and much more in terms of care.

4. See the original French text at the website of the Project Gutenberg in Australia: http://gutenberg.net.au/ebooks03/0300771h.html (accessed September 2013).

5. See Westman (2001) and, more recently, De Wispelaere & Weinstock (2012).

6. If a restrictive licence would be too much to swallow, LaFollette suggests that the licence could be redesigned to act as an incentive rather than a prohibition. As an analogy he takes the practice of certain car insurance companies of offering advanced driving tests to teenagers, i.e. tests that would be more stringent than the legally required test. If the teenager passes this stringent test, then his subsequent insurance premiums are reduced. In a similar way, claims LaFollette, parents could be offered greater financial support in return for successfully applying for the parenting licence, even though those without the licence would go unpenalized as under the present system.

7. RESPONSIBILITY FOR STRANGERS

1. There is an enormous literature on political identity, community and recognition. A good place to start would be Cressida Heyes's entry "Identity Politics" in the online *Stanford Encyclopedia of Philosophy* (http://plato. stanford.edu, accessed September 2013).

2. See his famous 1972 essay, "Famine, Affluence and Morality".

3. For an argument against relying too much on literary examples, see O'Neill (1986).

4. All quotations are taken from chapter XVI of an online version of Mark Twain's *Huckleberry Finn* at the *Project Gutenburg* website: www.gutenberg.org/files/76/76-h/76-h.htm (accessed September 2013).

5. For completeness, I should mention that the Bennett–Goldman debate shares many aspects with the much longer and deeper and greatly ramified debate between Humean and Kantian conceptions of the fundamental nature of morality, moral experience and moral disagreement. I do not, however, want to get bogged down in Hume and Kant, or in their terminology and assumptions. Lara Denis's entry on "Kant and Hume on Morality" in the online *Stanford Encyclopedia of Philosophy* (http://plato.stanford.edu) is the best place to start on this (accessed September 2013).

6. Williams earlier approached the inverse concept, "practical necessity" in his volume *Moral Luck* (1981a).

7. In a response to Williams, Ton Van den Beld (1997: 529) discusses the Luther example, and explains that the famous quotation was actually followed by Luther saying "So help me God". This, argues Van den Beld, suggests that Luther was asking God for help in making a commitment and sticking by it, rather than declaring an incapacity.

8. For completeness, I should mention that Taylor wrote *two* articles against Williams. The first, "Moral Incapacity" (1995), argued against Williams's insistence on implied deliberation, but did not mention Huck. Williams was then defended against Taylor by Michael Clark (1999). Taylor then responded to Clark (and again to Williams) in 2001, and here invoked the Huck example. It is from this last article that I will be citing.

9. My argument against Goldman draws inspiration from another article by Bernard Williams, "Internal and External Reasons" (1981c). Also see Ch. 8 n. 3, below.

8. LEARNING TO LOVE

1. According to one popular theory of love, love involves bestowing value where there was no value before (see Kolodny 2003). The debate about the nature of love is not sufficiently relevant here because that debate is mainly about what it means to love a person (with occasional references to loving animals, or countries, or cars). There is not much discussion about loving a situation.

2. In his review of an earlier draft of this book.

3. In this I am accepting the argument of Bernard Williams's "reasons-internalism". Williams asks what it means for a person to have a reason to do something. Roughly, a person has an "internal" reason if he is already consciously aware of that reason, or if he reliably would become aware of it if he corrected relevant mistaken factual beliefs and inferences. An external reason to do something is a reason which applies to the agent *even if* he

is not aware of the reason, does not accept it when he is told it, and does not have any way of getting to a position of accepting the reason. Williams denies that there are any genuinely external reasons; that what are called external reasons are merely reasons that one person launches at the other in the mere hope that they will be accepted and motivate the agent internally. See Williams (1981c). For a defence of Williams against three different critics, see Cowley (2005).

4. There is a question of whether the wife has to learn to love her husband, or her situation. In terms of the phenomenology of her experience, it is the husband who must be the first object of love: if she can learn to love him, the other aspects of the situation will fall into place. On the other hand, learning to love the situation in the abstract would not necessarily lead to loving *this* particular man.

5. For an overview of the problems of self-deception, see Ian Deweese-Boyd's entry "Self-deception" in the online *Stanford Encyclopedia of Philosophy* (http://plato.stanford.edu, accessed September 2013).

6. I have avoided the case of spousal abuse because of the additional complexity that would prevent a proper treatment here. I am merely interested in the question of what the wife should do, given her dislike for her husband.

BIBLIOGRAPHY

Arendt, H. [1963] 2011. *Eichmann in Jerusalem: A Report on the Banality of Evil.* New York: Tantor Media.

Austin, J. L. 1956. "A Plea for Excuses: The Presidential Address." *Proceedings of the Aristotelian Society* 57: 1–30.

Barnum-Roberts, B. 2011. "Apologizing Without Regret". *Ratio* (New Series) 24: 17–27.

Bennett, C. 2004. "The Limits of Mercy". *Ratio* (New Series) 17: 1–11.

Bennett, J. 1974. "The Conscience of Huckleberry Finn". *Philosophy* 49: 123–34.

Blustein, J. 2000. "On Taking Responsibility for One's Past". *Journal of Applied Philosophy* 17(1): 1–19.

Brown, A. 2009. *Personal Responsibility: Why it Matters.* London: Continuum.

Clark, M. 1999. "Moral Incapacity and Deliberation". *Ratio* 12: 1–13.

Cowley, C. 2005. "A New Defence of Williams's Reasons-Internalism". *Philosophical Investigations* 28(4): 346–68.

Cowley, C. 2008. *Medical Ethics: Ordinary Concepts, Ordinary Lives.* Basingstoke: Palgrave Macmillan.

Cowley, C. 2010. "Why Genuine Forgiveness must be Elective and Unconditional". *Ethical Perspectives* 17(4): 556–79.

Cowley, C. 2011. "Learning to Love". *Philosophical Topics* 38(1): 1–15.

De Wispelaere, J. & D. Weinstock 2012. "Licensing Parents to Protect Our Children?" *Ethics and Social Welfare* 6(2): 195–205.

Dennett, D. C. 1984. *Elbow Room: The Varieties of Free Will Worth Wanting.* Cambridge, MA: MIT Press.

Derrida, J. 2001. *On Cosmopolitanism and Forgiveness.* London: Routledge.

Duff, A. 2000. *Punishment, Communication, and Community.* New York: Oxford University Press.

Duff, A. 2005. "Who is Responsible, for What, to Whom?" *Ohio State Journal of Criminal Law* 2: 441–61.

Feinberg, J. 1965. "The Expressive Theory of Punishment". *Monist* 49: 397–423.

Feinberg, J. 1970. "What's So Special About Mental Illness?" In his *Doing and Deserving*, 272–92. Princeton, NJ: Princeton University Press.

Feinberg, J. 1995. "Equal Punishment for Failed Attempts: Some Bad but Instructive Arguments Against It". *Arizona Law Review* 37: 117–33.

Fischer, J. M. & M. Ravizza 1999. *Responsibility and Control: A Theory of Moral Responsibility*. Cambridge: Cambridge University Press.

Foot, P. 1977. "Abortion and the Doctrine of Double-effect". In her *Virtues and Vices and Other Essays in Moral Philosophy*, 19-32. Cambridge: Cambridge University Press.

Frankfurt, H. 1971. "Freedom of the Will and the Concept of a Person". *Journal of Philosophy* 68(1): 5–20. Reprinted in Frankfurt 1988.

Frankfurt, H. 1988. *The Importance of What We Care About: Philosophical Essays*. Cambridge: Cambridge University Press.

Frankfurt, H. 1998. "Duty and Love". *Philosophical Explorations* 1(1) 4–9.

Frankfurt, H. 1999. *Necessity, Volition, and Love*. Cambridge: Cambridge University Press.

Frisch, L. E. 1982. "On Licentious Licensing: A Reply to Hugh LaFollette". *Philosophy and Public Affairs* 11(2): 173–80.

Gaita, R. 2004. *Good and Evil: An Absolute Conception*. London: Routledge.

Garrard, E. & D. McNaughton 2003. "III – In Defence of Unconditional Forgiveness". In *Proceedings of the Aristotelian Society* 103(1): 39–60.

Goldman, A. 2010. "Huckleberry Finn and Moral Motivation". *Philosophy and Literature* 34:1–16.

Griswold, C. 2007. *Forgiveness: A Philosophical Exploration*. Cambridge: Cambridge University Press.

Hampton, J. 1984. "The Moral Education Theory of Punishment". *Philosophy and Public Affairs* 13(3): 208–38.

Holland, R. F. 1980. "Good and Evil in Action". In his *Against Empiricism: on Education, Epistemology and Value*, 110–25. Oxford: Blackwell.

James, W. 1979. *The Will to Believe and Other Essays in Popular Philosophy*. Cambridge, MA: Harvard University Press.

Kinnaman, T. 2005. "The Role of Character in Hume's Account of Moral Responsibility". *Journal of Value Inquiry* 39(1): 11–25.

Kolodny, N. 2003. "Love as Valuing a Relationship". *The Philosophical Review* 112(2): 135–89.

Kripke, S. 1980. *Naming and Necessity*. Cambridge, MA: Harvard University Press.

LaFollette, H. 1980. "Licensing Parents". *Philosophy and Public Affairs* 9(2): 182–97.

LaFollette, H. 2010. "Licensing Parents Revisited". *Journal of Applied Philosophy* 27(4): 327–43.

Lazare, A. 2005. *On Apology*. New York: Oxford University Press.

Le Sage, L. & D. De Ruyter 2008. "Criminal Parental Responsibility". *Educational Philosophy and Theory* 40(6): 789–802.

Levi, D. 1993. "What's Luck Got to Do With It?" In *Moral Luck*, D. Statman (ed.), 109–22. Albany, NY: SUNY Press.

Lucas, J. 1970. *The Freedom of the Will*. Oxford: Clarendon Press.

Mabbott, J. D. 1939. "Punishment". *Mind* (New Series) 48(190): 152–67.

MacIntyre, A. C. 1999. *Dependent Rational Animals: Why Human Beings Need the Virtues*. Cambridge: Cambridge University Press.

Mason, E. 2005. "Recent Work: Moral Responsibility". *Philosophical Books* 46(4): 343–53.

Mason, H. 1996. *Moral Dilemmas and Moral Theory*. Oxford: Oxford University Press.

Matravers, M. 2007. *Responsibility and Justice*. Cambridge: Polity.

Moody-Adams, M. 1993. "On the Old Saw that Character is Destiny". In *Identity, Character, and Morality: Essays in Moral Psychology*, O. J. Flanagan & A. O. Rorty (eds), 111–32. Cambridge, MA: MIT Press.

Murdoch, I. 1970. *The Sovereignty of Good*. London: Routledge & Kegan Paul.

Murphy, J. G. & J. Hampton 1990. *Forgiveness and Mercy*. Cambridge: Cambridge University Press.

Nagel, T. 1979. "Moral Luck". In his *Mortal Questions*, 24–38. Cambridge: Cambridge University Press.

Nietzsche, F. 1967. *Ecce Homo*. In *The Basic Writings of Nietzsche*, W. Kaufman (ed.), 655–801. New York: Random House.

Nussbaum, M. 1993. "Equity and Mercy". *Philosophy and Public Affairs* 22(2):83–125.

O'Neill, O. 1986."The Power of Example". *Philosophy* 61(235): 5–29.

Parfit, D. 1984. *Reasons and Persons*. Oxford: Oxford University Press.

Phillips, D. Z. 1992. *Interventions in Ethics*. Albany, NY: SUNY Press.

Pettigrove, G. & J. Collins. 2011. "Apologizing for Who I Am". *Journal of Applied Philosophy* 28(2): 137–50.

Richards, N. 1993. "Luck and Desert". In *Moral Luck*, D. Statman (ed.), 167–80. Albany, NY: SUNY Press.

Sartre, J.-P. 1993. *Essays in Existentialism*. New York: Citadel Press.

Sartre, J.-P. [1946] 2005. "Existentialism is a Humanism." P. Mairet (trans.). www.marxists.org/reference/archive/sartre/works/exist/sartre.htm (accessed September 2013).

Sher, G. 2009. *Who Knew? Responsibility Without Awareness*. New York: Oxford University Press.

Singer, P. 1972. "Famine, Affluence and Morality". *Philosophy and Public Affairs* 1: 229–43.

Smart, J. & B. Williams 1973. *Utilitarianism: For and Against*. Cambridge: Cambridge University Press.

Smith, A. 2008. "Control, Responsibility and Moral Assessment". *Philosophical Studies* 138: 367–92.

Smith, N. 2008. *I was Wrong: The Meanings of Apologies*. Cambridge: Cambridge University Press.

Speer, A. 1970. *Inside the Third Reich*. New York: Macmillan.

Speer, A. 1976. *Spandau: The Secret Diaries*. New York: Macmillan.

Statman, D. (ed.) 1993. *Moral Luck*. Albany, NY: SUNY Press.

Stocker, M. 1999. "Responsibility and the Abuse Excuse". *Social Philosophy and Policy* 16(2): 175–200.

Strawson, P. F. 2008. *Freedom and Resentment and Other Essays*. London: Routledge.

Styron, W. 1979. *Sophie's Choice*. London: Random House.

Tasioulas, J. 2003. "Mercy". *Proceedings of the Aristotelian Society* 103(1): 101–32.

Taylor, C. 1995. "Moral Incapacity". *Philosophy* 70: 273–85.

Taylor, C. 2001. "Moral Incapacity and Huckleberry Finn". *Philosophy* 76: 56–67.

Thomson, J. J. 1971. "A Defense of Abortion". *Philosophy & Public Affairs* 1: 47–66.

Thomson, J. J. 1991. "Self-defense". *Philosophy & Public Affairs* 20(4): 283–310.

Van den Beld, T. 1997. "Moral Incapacities". *Philosophy* 72: 525–36.

Watson G. 1996. "Two Faces of Responsibility". *Philosophical Topics* 24(2): 227–48.

Westman, J. C. 2001. *Licensing Parents: Can We Prevent Child Abuse and Neglect?* New York: Da Capo Press.

Williams, B. 1981a. *Moral Luck: Philosophical Papers 1973–1980*. Cambridge: Cambridge University Press.

Williams, B. 1981b. "Practical Necessity". In his *Moral Luck: Philosophical Papers 1973–1980*, 124–31. Cambridge: Cambridge University Press.

Williams, B. 1981c. "Internal and External Reasons". In his *Moral Luck: Philosophical Papers 1973–1980*, 101–13. Cambridge: Cambridge University Press.

Williams, B. 1981d. "Moral Luck". In his *Moral Luck: Philosophical Papers 1973–1980*, 20–39. Cambridge: Cambridge University Press.

Williams, B. 1995. "Moral Incapacity". In his *Making Sense of Humanity*, 46–55. Cambridge: Cambridge University Press.

Williams, B. 2011. *Ethics and the Limits of Philosophy*, 2nd edn. London: Routledge.

Williams, G. 2013. "Sharing Responsibility and Holding Responsible". *Journal of Applied Philosophy*. http://onlinelibrary.wiley.com/doi/10.1111/japp.12019/abstract ("early view"; accessed September 2013).

Winch, P. 1972. "Ethical Reward and Punishment". In his *Ethics and Action*, 210–27. London: Macmillan.

Winch, P. 1987. "Who is my Neighbour?" In his *Trying to Make Sense*, 154–60. Oxford: Blackwell.

Wolf, S. 1993. *Freedom within Reason*. New York: Oxford University Press.

INDEX